PHILIP'S ROAD

CONCISE BRITAIN

II	**Key to road map symbols**
III	**Distance table**
IV	**Counties map**
1	**Key to map pages**
2	**Road maps of Great Britain** at 8 miles to 1 inch
58	**Road maps of Ireland** at 19 miles to 1 inch
62	**Index to road maps of Ireland**
64	**Index to road maps of Great Britain**

www.philips-maps.co.uk

First published in 2010 by Philip's
a division of Octopus Publishing Group Ltd
www.octopusbooks.co.uk
Carmelite House, 50 Victoria Embankment
London EC4Y 0DZ
An Hachette UK Company
www.hachette.co.uk

Fourth edition 2019, first impression 2019
ISBN 978-1-84907-507-7

Cartography by Philip's, copyright © 2019 Philip's

This product includes mapping data licensed
from Ordnance Survey®, with the permission
of the Controller of Her Majesty's Stationery
Office. © Crown copyright 2019. All rights
reserved. Licence number 100011710

The map of Ireland on pages 58–61 is based
upon the Crown Copyright and is reproduced
with the permission of Land & Property
Services under delegated authority from the
Controller of Her Majesty's Stationery Office, © Crown Copyright
and database right 2019, PMLPA No 100503, and on
Ordnance Survey Ireland by permission of the Government
© Ordnance Survey Ireland / Government of Ireland
Permit number 9181.

Printed in China

*Nielsen BookScan Travel Publishing Year Book 2017 data

Road map symbols

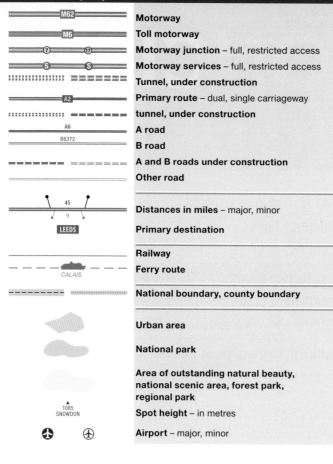

M62	Motorway
M6	Toll motorway
⑦ ⑰	Motorway junction – full, restricted access
Ⓢ Ⓢ	Motorway services – full, restricted access
	Tunnel, under construction
A2	Primary route – dual, single carriageway
	tunnel, under construction
A6	A road
B6372	B road
	A and B roads under construction
	Other road
45 / 9	Distances in miles – major, minor
LEEDS	Primary destination
	Railway
CALAIS	Ferry route
	National boundary, county boundary
	Urban area
	National park
	Area of outstanding natural beauty, national scenic area, forest park, regional park
▲ 1085 SNOWDON	Spot height – in metres
✈ ✈	Airport – major, minor

Scales

Pages 2–56
1:506880, 1cm = 5.07 km, 1 in = 8 miles

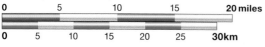

| 0 | 5 | 10 | 15 | **20 miles** |
| 0 | 5 | 10 | 15 | 20 | 25 | **30km** |

Pages 58–61
1:1200000, 1cm = 12km, 1 in = 18.94 miles

| 0 | 10 | 20 | **30 miles** |
| 0 | 10 | 20 | 30 | 40 | **50km** |

Abbreviated local authority areas

BD	Bridgend	13 G12
BF	Bracknell Forest	16 J3
BG	Blaenau Gwent	13 E15
BL	Blackpool	26 B4
BM	Bournemouth	8 H5
BN	Blackburn with Darwen	27 C8
CB	City and County of Bristol	14 J4
CBH	City of Brighton and Hove	10 J3
CE	City of Edinburgh	40 F5
CF	Cardiff	7 C10
CM	Clackmannanshire	40 D2
CN	City of Nottingham	22 A4
CY	Caerphilly	7 B10
DD	Dundee City	51 P3
DE	Derby City	22 B2
DN	Darlington	32 C4
ED	East Dunbartonshire	39 C11
ER	East Renfrewshire	39 E9
FK	Falkirk	39 C13
GC	Glasgow City	39 D10
HL	Hartlepool	32 A6
HN	Halton	26 G6
IC	Inverclyde	39 D8
KH	Kingston upon Hull	29 A9
LE	Leicester City	22 E5
LU	Luton	16 C5
MB	Middlesbrough	32 C6
MR	Merthyr Tydfil	13 E14
NEL	North East Lincolnshire	29 D11
NL	North Lanarkshire	39 D13
NP	Newport	7 C12
NPT	Neath Port Talbot	13 F11
PL	Plymouth	3 F12
PM	Portsmouth	9 G11
PO	Poole	8 H5
RC	Redcar and Cleveland	33 C8
RD	Reading	16 H2
RF	Renfrewshire	39 D9
RT	Rhondda Cynon Taff	7 B9
SD	Southend-on-Sea	17 G14
SL	Slough	16 G4
SN	Stockton-on-Tees	32 B6
SO	Southampton	9 F9
ST	Stoke-on-Trent	21 A9
SW	Swindon	15 G10
TB	Torbay	4 G2
TF	Torfaen	7 A11
TK	Thurrock	17 G12
TW	Telford and Wrekin	20 E7
WA	Warrington	26 G7
WD	West Dunbartonshire	39 C9
WK	Wokingham	16 J2
WL	West Lothian	40 F3
WM	Windsor and Maidenhead	16 H3

Distance table

How to use this table

Distances are shown in miles and, in light type, kilometres. For example, the distance between Birmingham and Dover is **194** miles or **312** kilometres.

London
517
832 **Aberdeen**
211 445
340 716 **Aberystwyth**
117 420 114
188 676 183 **Birmingham**
107 564 207 147
172 908 333 237 **Bournemouth**
52 573 253 163 92
84 922 407 262 148 **Brighton**
122 493 125 81 82 147
196 793 201 130 132 237 **Bristol**
54 471 214 100 154 116 169
87 758 344 161 248 187 272 **Cambridge**
157 505 105 103 117 182 45 190
253 813 169 166 188 293 72 306 **Cardiff**
301 221 224 196 343 370 277 264 289
484 356 360 315 552 596 446 425 465 **Carlisle**
71 588 297 194 174 82 202 125 238 389
114 947 478 312 280 132 325 201 383 626 **Dover**
448 67 376 349 495 517 430 406 441 152 523
721 108 605 562 797 832 692 654 710 245 842 **Dundee**
390 125 320 292 439 456 373 345 385 96 462 56
628 201 515 470 707 734 600 555 620 154 744 90 **Edinburgh**
260 504 56 170 222 291 154 270 112 297 331 460 399
418 811 90 274 357 468 248 435 180 478 533 740 642 **Fishguard**
510 149 430 392 539 575 486 479 485 206 596 127 144 486
821 240 692 631 867 926 782 771 781 332 959 204 232 782 **Fort William**
397 145 320 292 439 468 373 372 385 96 488 83 44 376 101
639 233 515 470 707 753 600 599 620 154 786 134 71 605 163 **Glasgow**
109 468 102 56 99 159 35 123 56 247 191 410 349 153 454 346
175 753 164 90 159 256 56 198 90 398 307 660 562 246 731 557 **Gloucester**
76 535 281 167 187 128 217 67 246 336 125 469 413 337 543 432 196
122 861 452 269 301 206 349 108 396 541 201 755 665 542 874 695 316 **Harwich**
269 439 111 148 288 334 206 270 216 231 360 394 333 167 438 330 191 349
433 707 179 238 463 538 332 435 348 372 580 634 536 269 705 531 307 562 **Holyhead**
550 105 486 458 597 617 539 505 549 262 622 132 158 542 66 166 504 569 474
885 169 782 737 961 993 867 813 884 422 1001 212 254 872 106 267 811 916 763 **Inverness**
663 232 601 574 724 741 668 630 680 391 746 259 285 671 191 259 628 693 603 129
1067 373 967 924 1165 1193 1075 1014 1094 629 1201 417 459 1080 307 417 1011 1116 970 208 **John o' Groats**
184 364 223 134 264 245 233 139 244 158 256 295 234 280 369 254 169 196 231 394 518
296 586 359 216 425 394 375 224 393 254 412 475 377 451 594 409 272 316 372 634 834 **Kingston upon Hull**
297 692 313 281 205 308 200 374 245 477 381 642 574 353 686 573 235 390 405 741 868 421
478 1114 504 452 330 496 322 602 394 768 613 1033 924 568 1104 922 378 628 652 1193 1397 678 **Land's End**
189 327 169 113 255 260 194 145 232 119 260 258 202 237 329 215 174 223 176 360 487 55 405
304 526 272 182 410 419 312 233 373 192 418 415 325 381 530 346 280 359 283 579 784 89 652 **Leeds**
131 383 199 90 209 197 183 85 208 191 202 314 258 272 399 291 159 155 216 427 554 44 371 68
211 616 320 145 336 317 295 137 335 307 325 505 415 438 642 468 256 249 348 687 892 71 597 109 **Lincoln**
202 341 104 93 234 272 161 194 169 120 299 286 216 160 329 216 140 265 102 382 511 130 361 75 129
325 549 167 150 377 438 259 312 272 193 481 460 348 257 530 348 225 427 164 615 822 209 581 121 208 **Liverpool**
185 340 129 80 227 257 161 165 183 119 276 285 215 197 329 215 126 228 124 373 500 95 361 40 84 35
298 547 208 129 365 414 259 266 295 192 444 459 346 317 530 346 203 367 200 600 805 153 581 64 135 56 **Manchester**
286 235 257 207 347 352 299 241 325 57 358 166 110 329 253 148 266 308 272 268 395 132 498 92 159 168 132
460 378 414 333 558 567 481 388 523 92 576 267 177 529 407 238 428 496 438 431 636 212 802 148 256 270 212 **Newcastle upon Tyne**
114 496 276 166 214 175 252 62 262 289 174 422 366 352 504 385 204 73 311 529 654 149 421 176 105 220 185 264
183 798 444 267 344 282 406 100 422 465 280 679 589 567 811 620 328 117 501 852 1053 240 678 283 169 354 298 425 **Norwich**
57 483 154 64 90 108 74 83 108 260 141 433 372 205 472 356 52 145 238 532 656 192 274 168 137 172 144 260 145
92 777 248 103 145 174 119 134 174 418 227 697 599 330 760 573 84 233 383 856 1056 309 441 270 221 277 232 418 233 **Oxford**
218 615 237 203 128 224 122 293 167 399 300 552 496 264 595 495 157 309 328 664 790 355 89 316 293 283 283 410 343 199
351 990 381 327 206 361 196 472 269 642 483 888 798 425 958 797 253 497 528 1069 1271 571 143 509 472 455 455 660 552 320 **Plymouth**
159 360 159 76 216 226 161 120 194 152 245 291 235 215 348 248 126 187 168 393 520 65 361 33 46 72 38 125 146 135 283
256 579 256 122 348 364 259 193 312 245 394 468 378 346 560 399 203 301 270 632 837 105 581 53 74 116 61 201 235 217 455 **Sheffield**
77 547 201 128 31 61 76 148 121 324 143 500 438 233 541 433 105 164 293 598 723 256 228 232 204 239 221 324 206 64 151 199
124 880 323 206 50 98 122 238 195 521 230 805 705 375 871 697 169 264 472 963 1164 412 367 373 328 385 356 521 332 103 243 320 **Southampton**
402 228 325 297 444 475 378 379 390 101 496 167 124 392 195 84 343 410 338 262 379 259 585 220 298 221 220 158 403 379 500 263 445
647 367 523 478 715 765 608 610 628 163 798 269 200 631 314 135 552 660 544 422 610 417 942 354 480 356 354 254 649 610 805 423 716 **Stranraer**
194 507 73 119 167 222 85 227 41 293 274 473 412 254 496 409 89 267 184 572 696 264 285 248 233 195 187 347 301 141 206 217 161 417
312 816 117 192 269 357 137 365 66 471 441 761 663 408 798 658 143 430 296 921 1120 425 459 399 375 314 301 559 485 227 332 349 259 671 **Swansea**
207 319 195 130 269 275 222 165 244 121 282 250 194 261 330 217 189 228 204 352 479 37 411 24 75 99 64 84 181 161 333 52 258 222 272
333 513 314 209 433 443 357 266 393 195 454 402 312 420 531 349 304 367 328 566 771 60 661 39 121 159 103 135 291 259 536 84 415 357 438 **York**

Map locations shown: John o' Groats, Inverness, Aberdeen, Fort William, Dundee, Glasgow, Edinburgh, Stranraer, Newcastle upon Tyne, Carlisle, York, Leeds, Manchester, Kingston upon Hull, Lincoln, Holyhead, Liverpool, Sheffield, Norwich, Birmingham, Aberystwyth, Cambridge, Fishguard, Swansea, Gloucester, Oxford, Harwich, Cardiff, Bristol, London, Dover, Southampton, Brighton, Bournemouth, Plymouth, Land's End.

Counties and unitary authorities

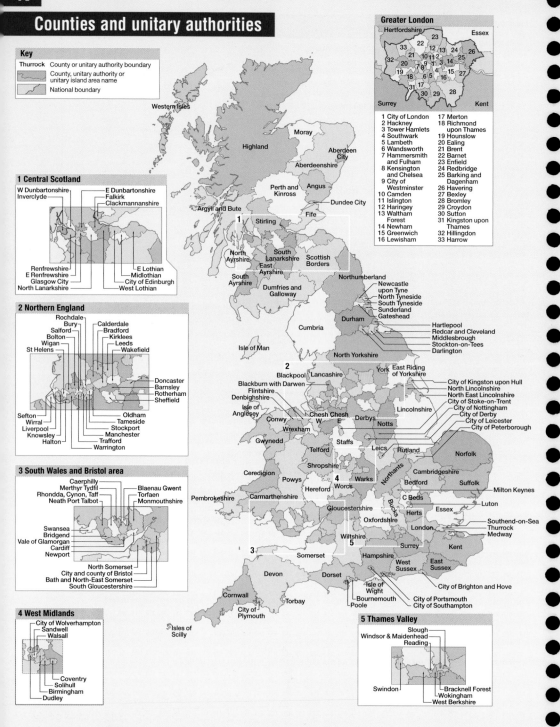

Key

Thurrock	County or unitary authority boundary
	County, unitary authority or unitary island area name
	National boundary

Greater London

Hertfordshire
Essex
Surrey
Kent

1 City of London
2 Hackney
3 Tower Hamlets
4 Southwark
5 Lambeth
6 Wandsworth
7 Hammersmith and Fulham
8 Kensington and Chelsea
9 City of Westminster
10 Camden
11 Islington
12 Haringey
13 Waltham Forest
14 Newham
15 Greenwich
16 Lewisham
17 Merton
18 Richmond upon Thames
19 Hounslow
20 Ealing
21 Brent
22 Barnet
23 Enfield
24 Redbridge
25 Barking and Dagenham
26 Havering
27 Bexley
28 Bromley
29 Croydon
30 Sutton
31 Kingston upon Thames
32 Hillingdon
33 Harrow

1 Central Scotland

W Dunbartonshire
Inverclyde
E Dunbartonshire
Falkirk
Clackmannanshire
Renfrewshire
E Renfrewshire
Glasgow City
North Lanarkshire
E Lothian
Midlothian
City of Edinburgh
West Lothian

2 Northern England

Rochdale
Bury
Salford
Bolton
Wigan
St Helens
Calderdale
Bradford
Kirklees
Leeds
Wakefield
Doncaster
Barnsley
Rotherham
Sheffield
Sefton
Wirral
Liverpool
Knowsley
Halton
Oldham
Tameside
Stockport
Manchester
Trafford
Warrington

3 South Wales and Bristol area

Caerphilly
Merthyr Tydfil
Rhondda, Cynon, Taff
Neath Port Talbot
Blaenau Gwent
Torfaen
Monmouthshire
Swansea
Bridgend
Vale of Glamorgan
Cardiff
Newport
North Somerset
City and county of Bristol
Bath and North-East Somerset
South Gloucestershire

4 West Midlands

City of Wolverhampton
Sandwell
Walsall
Coventry
Solihull
Birmingham
Dudley

5 Thames Valley

Slough
Windsor & Maidenhead
Reading
Swindon
Bracknell Forest
Wokingham
West Berkshire

Western Isles
Moray
Highland
Aberdeen City
Aberdeenshire
Perth and Kinross
Angus
Argyll and Bute
Dundee City
Stirling
Fife
North Ayrshire
South Lanarkshire
East Ayrshire
Scottish Borders
South Ayrshire
Dumfries and Galloway
Northumberland
Newcastle upon Tyne
North Tyneside
South Tyneside
Sunderland
Gateshead
Durham
Hartlepool
Redcar and Cleveland
Middlesbrough
Stockton-on-Tees
Darlington
Cumbria
Isle of Man
North Yorkshire
York
East Riding of Yorkshire
City of Kingston upon Hull
North Lincolnshire
North East Lincolnshire
City of Stoke-on-Trent
City of Nottingham
City of Derby
City of Leicester
City of Peterborough
Blackpool
Lancashire
Blackburn with Darwen
Flintshire
Denbighshire
Isle of Anglesey
Conwy
Chesh W
Chesh E
Derbys
Notts
Lincolnshire
Wrexham
Gwynedd
Telford
Staffs
Leics
Rutland
Norfolk
Ceredigion
Shropshire
Powys
Warks
Northants
Cambridgeshire
Hereford
Worcs
Bedford
Suffolk
Milton Keynes
Pembrokeshire
Carmarthenshire
Gloucestershire
Bucks
C Beds
Luton
Herts
Essex
Oxfordshire
London
Southend-on-Sea
Thurrock
Medway
Wiltshire
Surrey
Kent
Somerset
Hampshire
West Sussex
East Sussex
Devon
Dorset
Isle of Wight
City of Brighton and Hove
Bournemouth
Poole
City of Portsmouth
City of Southampton
Cornwall
Torbay
City of Plymouth
Isles of Scilly

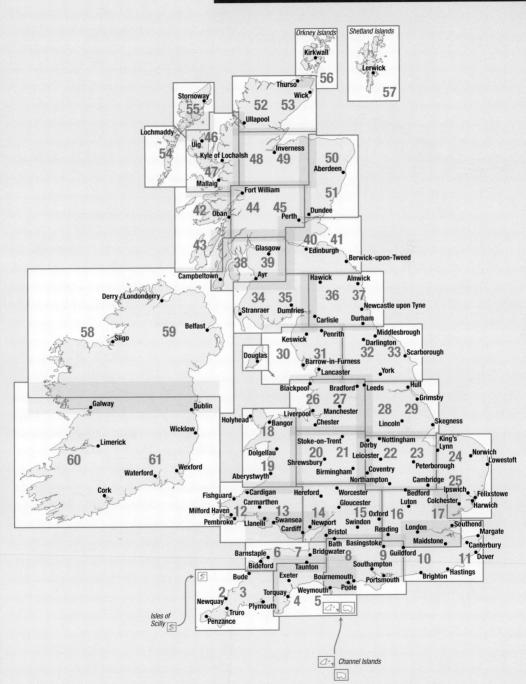

Orkney Islands

Kirkwall

56

Shetland Islands

Lerwick

57

Thurso
Wick

52 53

Stornoway

55

Ullapool

Lochmaddy

46
Uig
Kyle of Lochalsh

54

Inverness

48 49

50
Aberdeen

47
Mallaig

Fort William

51

44 45
Perth

Dundee

42
Oban

43

38 39
Glasgow
Ayr

Campbeltown

40 41
Edinburgh
Berwick-upon-Tweed

Derry / Londonderry

34 35
Stranraer Dumfries

Hawick
Alnwick

36 37
Newcastle upon Tyne

Carlisle
Durham

58
Sligo

59
Belfast

Keswick
Penrith

Middlesbrough
Darlington

30
Douglas

31
Barrow-in-Furness
Lancaster

32 33
Scarborough

York

Galway

Dublin

Blackpool

Bradford Leeds
Hull

26 27
Liverpool Manchester
Chester

28 29
Grimsby

Lincoln
Skegness

Wicklow

Holyhead

18
Bangor

Stoke-on-Trent

Derby Nottingham

King's
Lynn

Limerick

60

61
Wexford

Waterford

Cork

Fishguard

Dolgellau

19
Aberystwyth

20 21
Shrewsbury

Leicester

22 23
Coventry
Northampton

24
Norwich
Lowestoft

Cambridge

25
Ipswich
Felixstowe
Harwich

Cardigan
Carmarthen

Hereford

Worcester
Gloucester

Bedford
Luton

Colchester

Milford Haven
Pembroke

12
Llanelli

13
Swansea
Cardiff

14
Newport
Bristol

15
Swindon
Oxford

16
Reading

17
Southend
Margate

London
Maidstone
Canterbury
Dover

Barnstaple

6 7
Bridgwater

Bath Basingstoke

8

9
Guildford

10

11
Hastings

Bideford

Taunton

Southampton
Portsmouth

Brighton

Bude

Exeter
Bournemouth
Poole

2 3
Newquay
Truro

Torquay
Plymouth

4

Weymouth

5

*Isles of
Scilly*

Penzance

Channel Islands

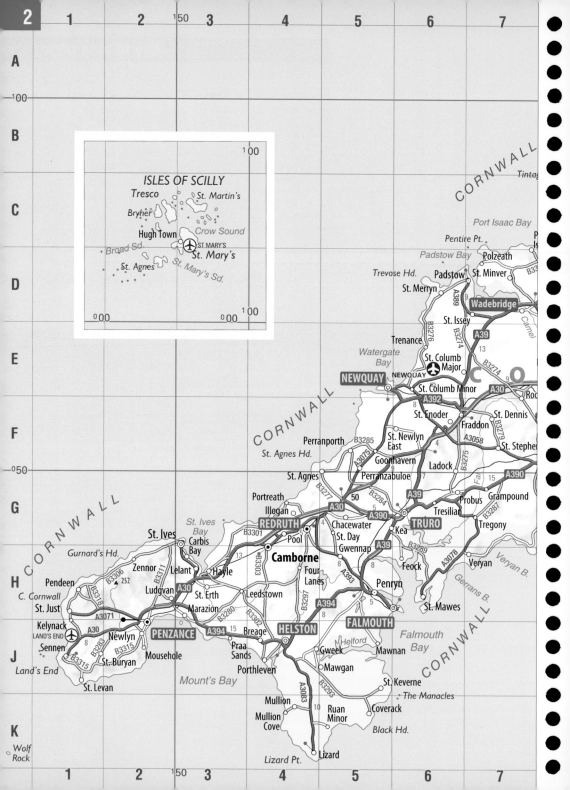

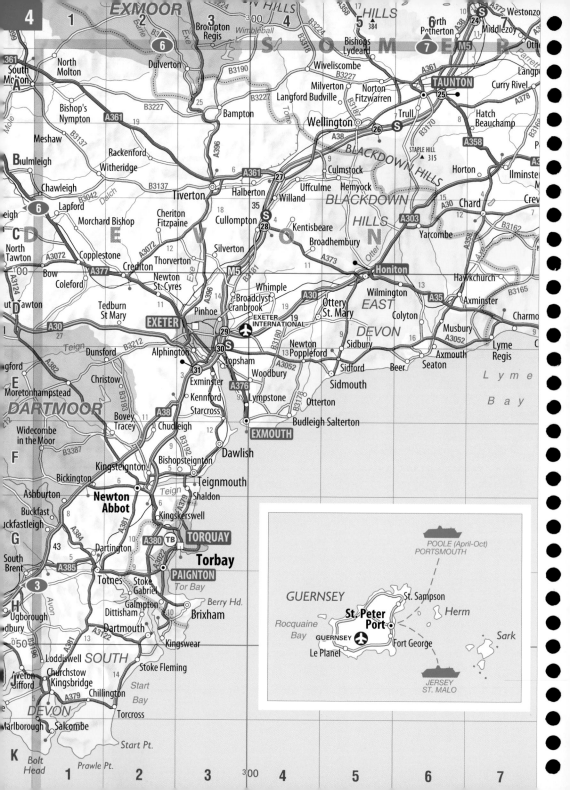

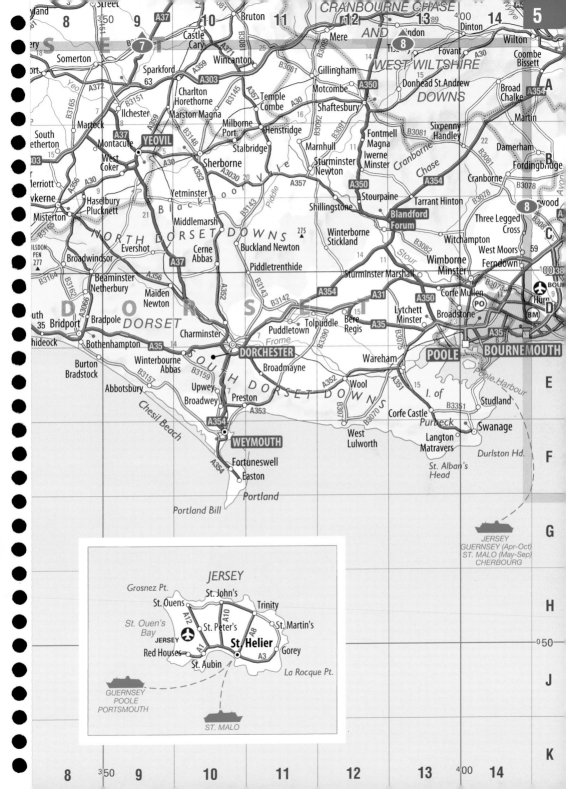

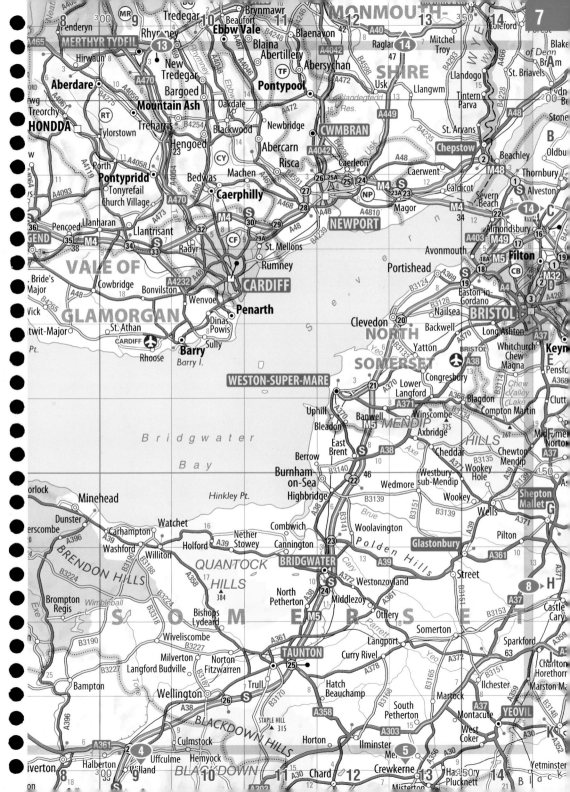

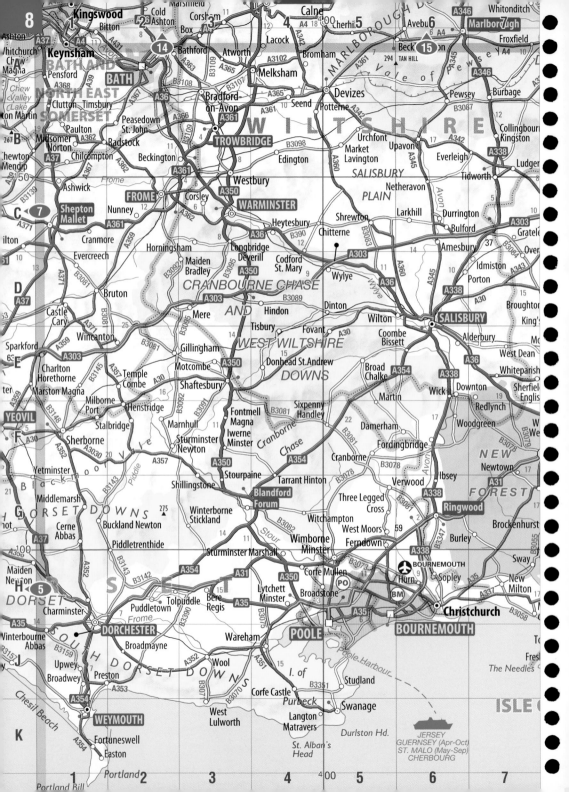

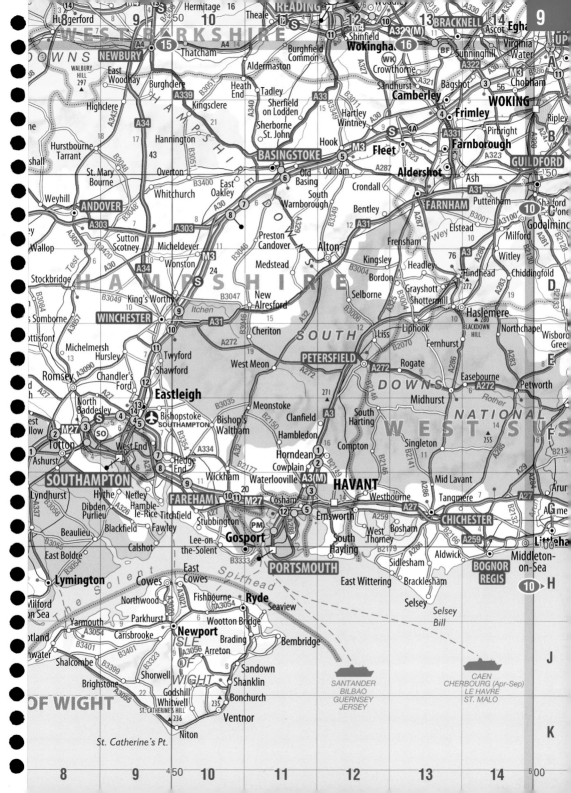

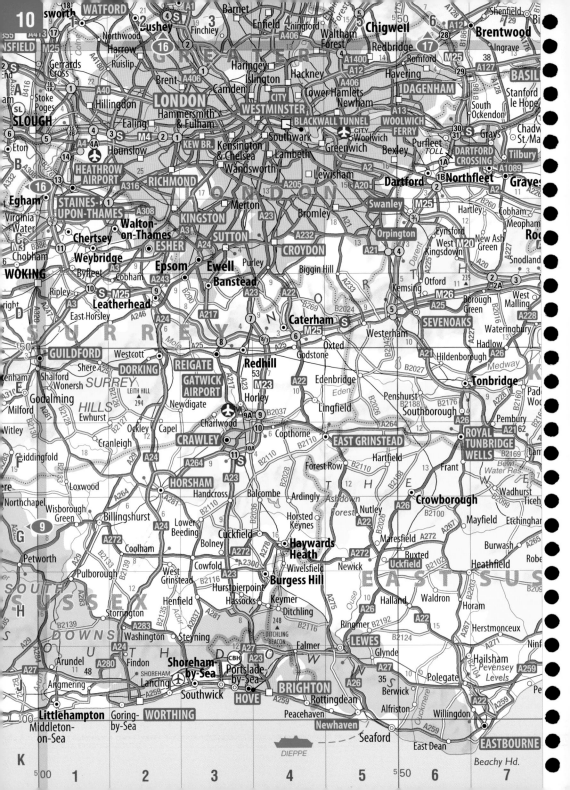

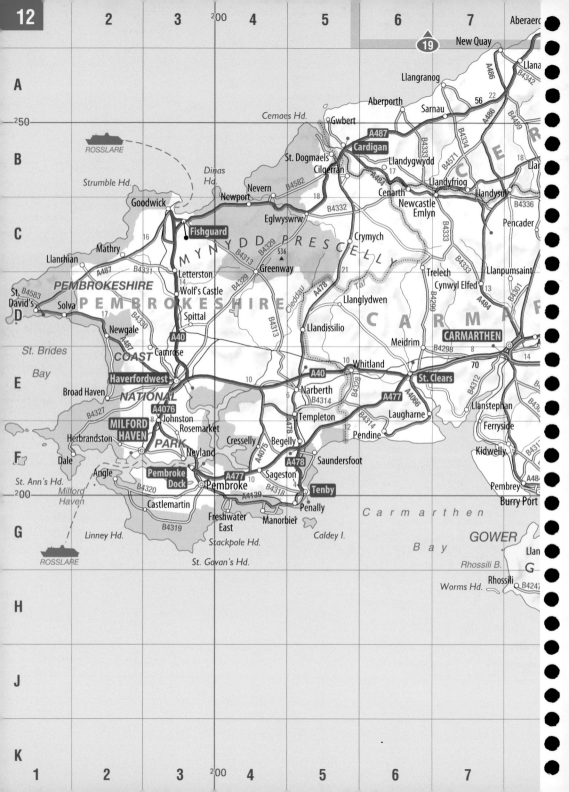

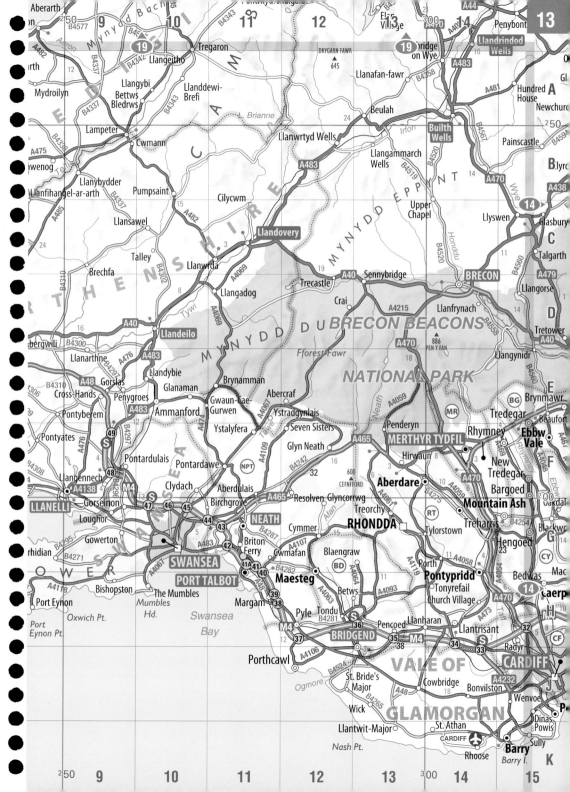

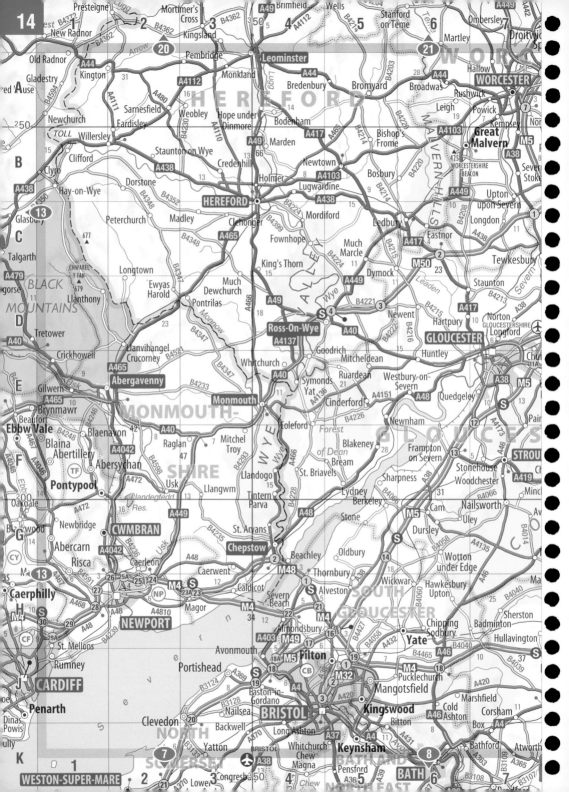

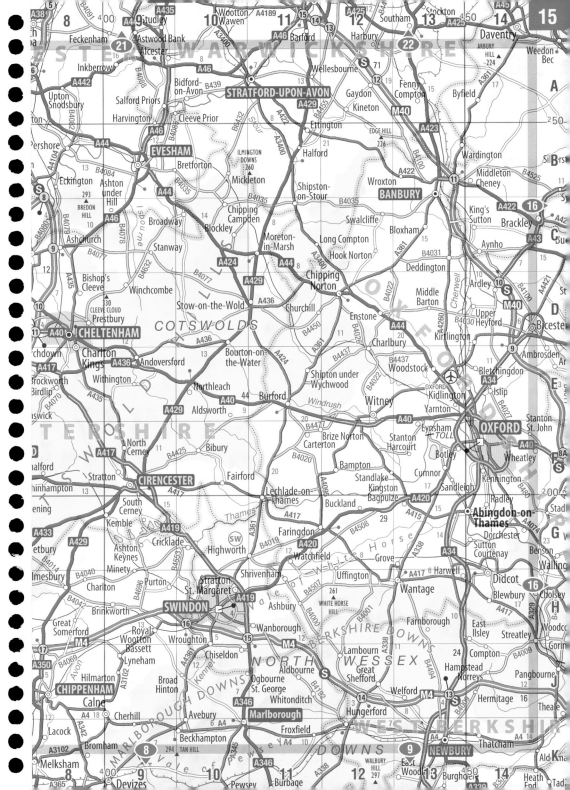

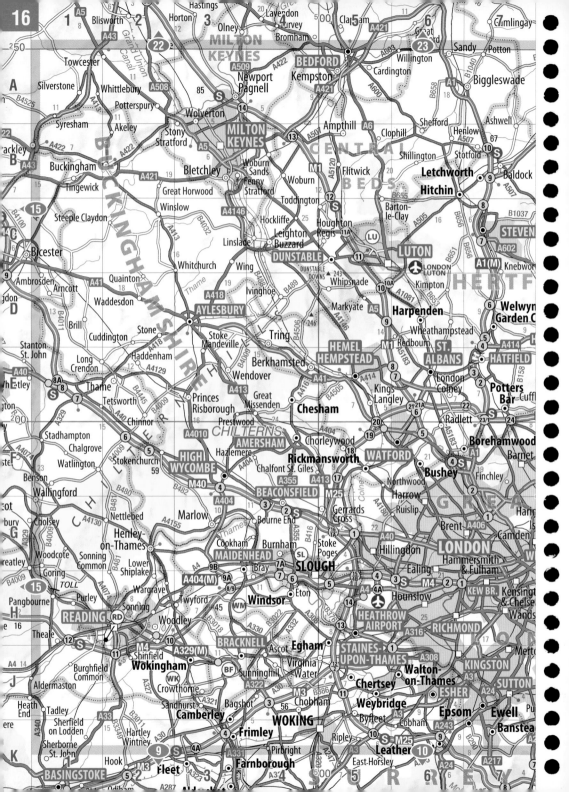

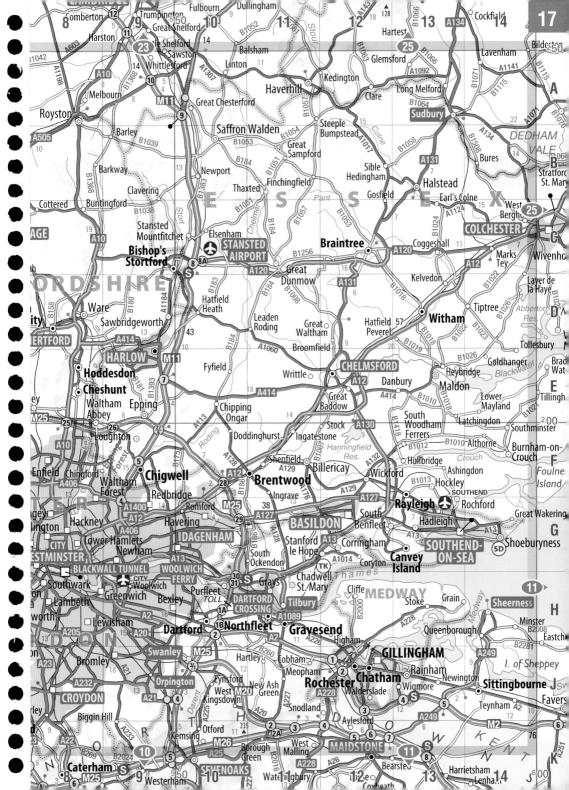

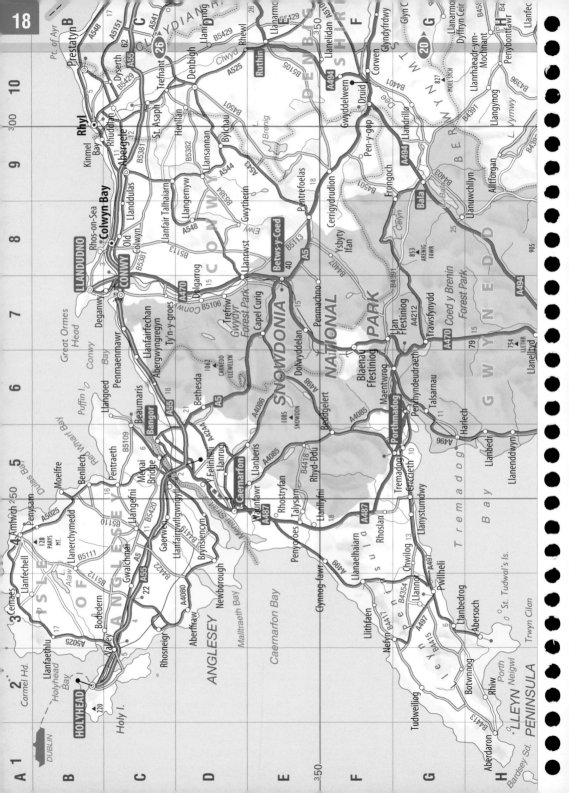

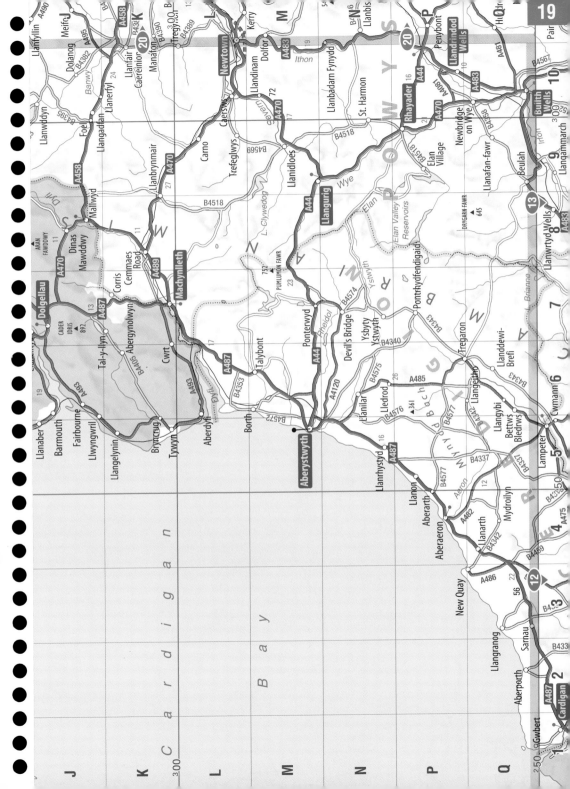

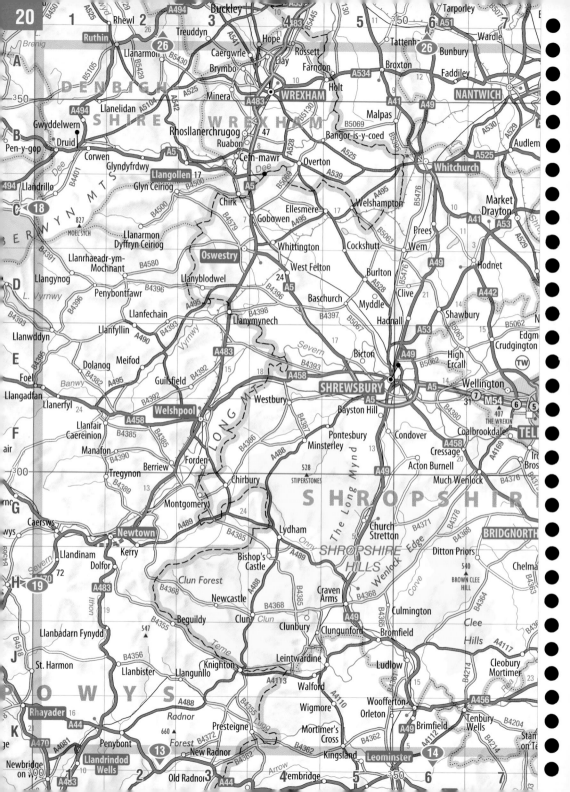

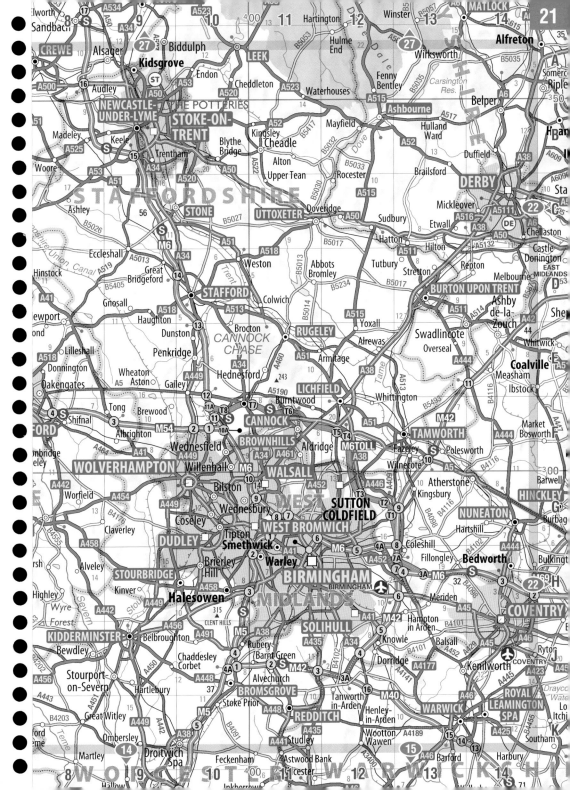

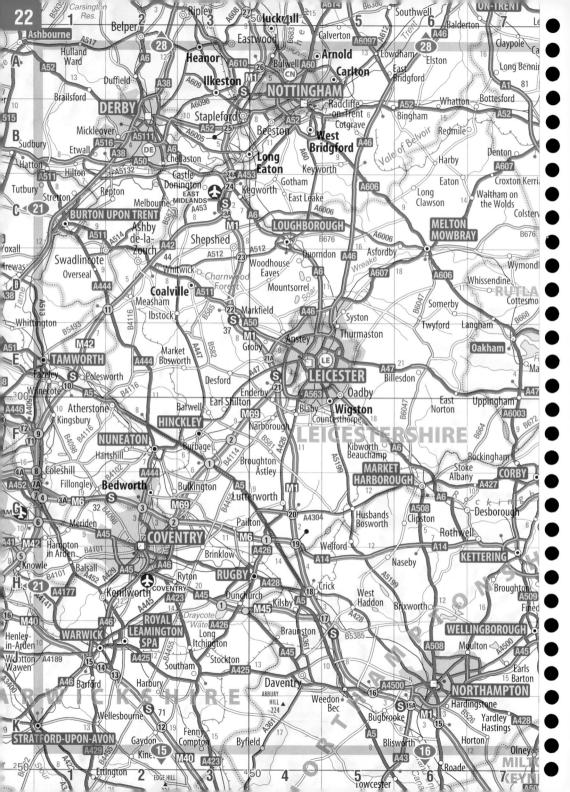

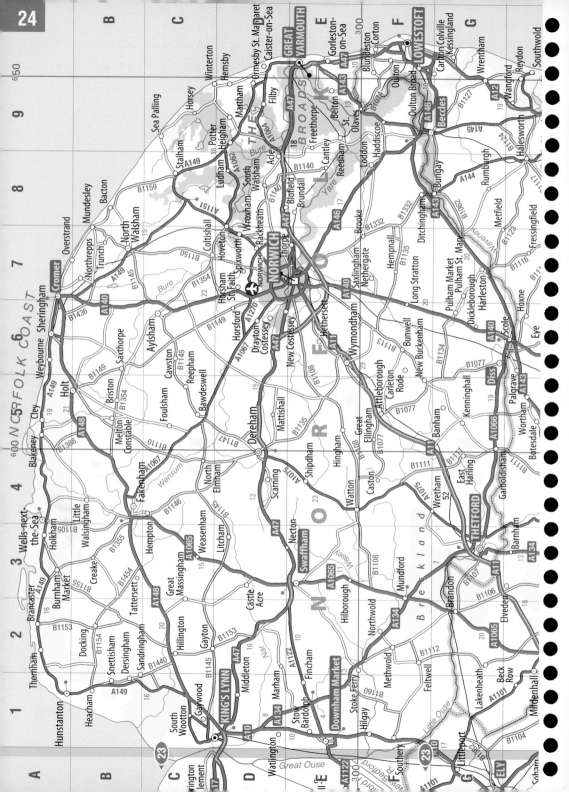

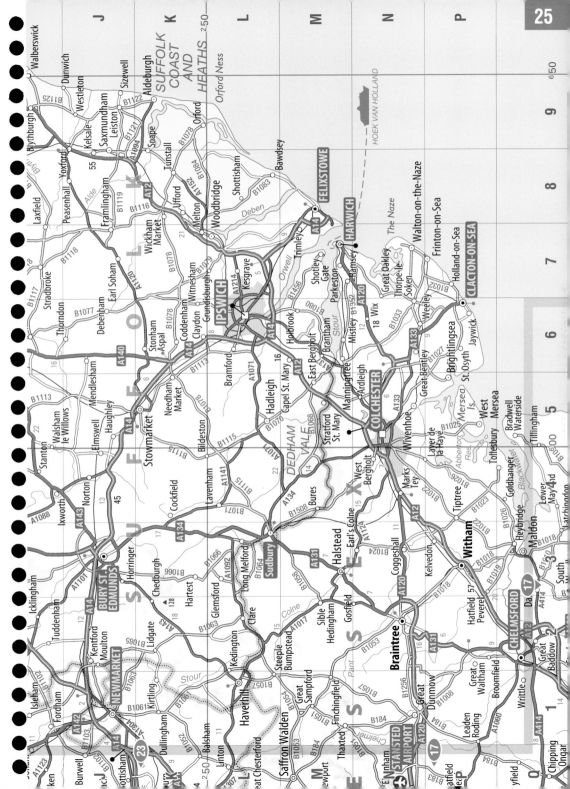

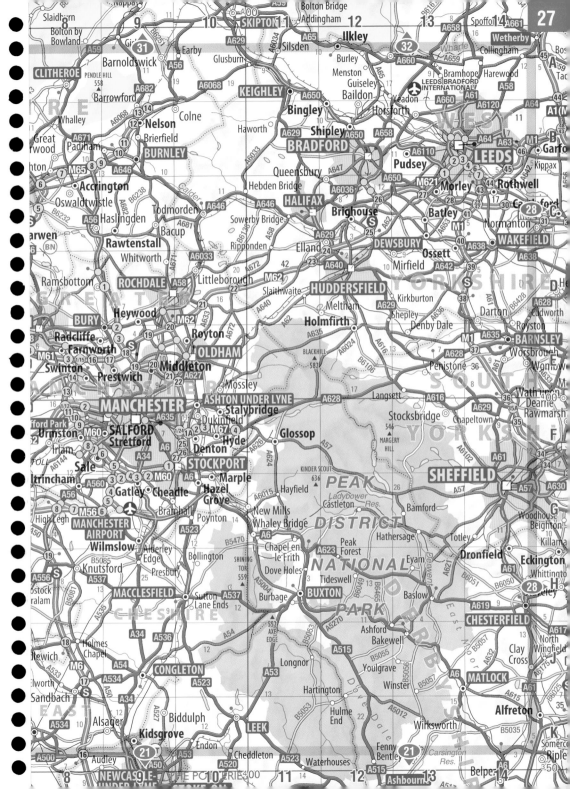

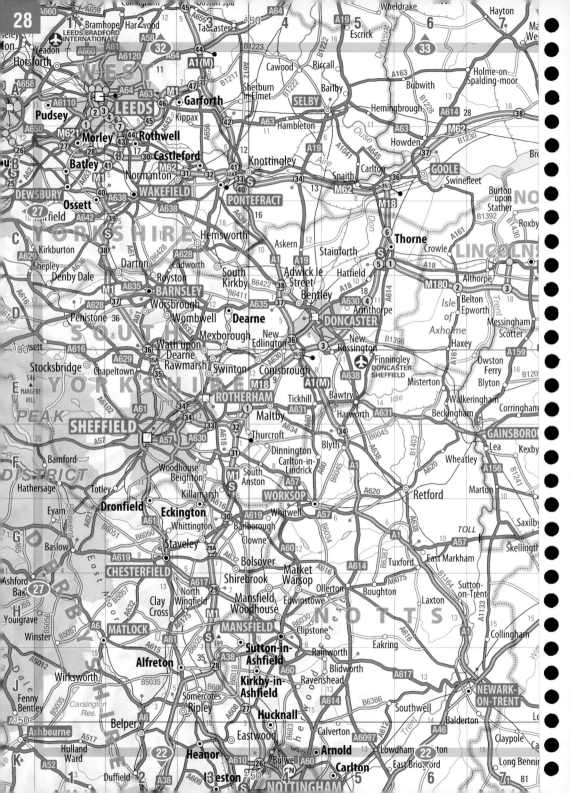

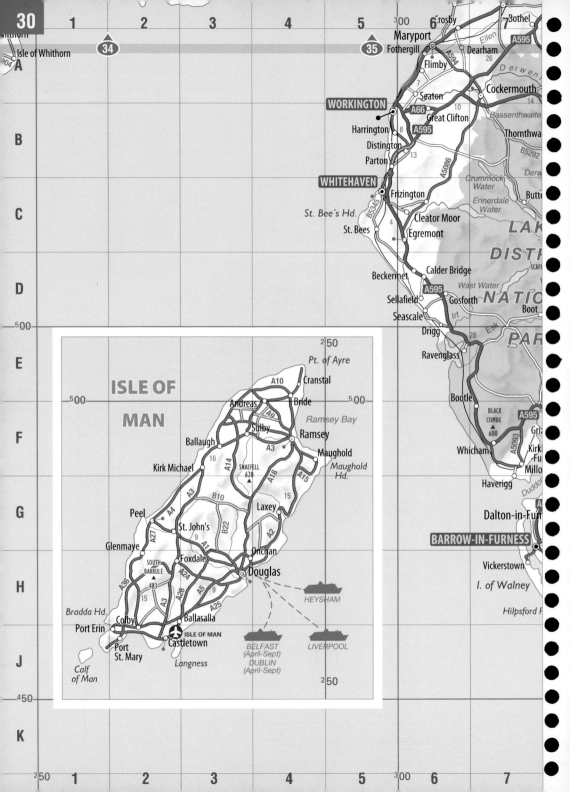

ISLE OF MAN

Isle of Whithorn

34

35

Maryport
Fothergill
Crosby
Bothel
Ellen
A595
Dearham
Flimby
Derwent
Seaton
Cockermouth
WORKINGTON
A66
Great Clifton
A595
Bassenthwaite
Harrington
Distington
Thornthwa
Parton
A5086
B5292
WHITEHAVEN
Frizington
Grummock Water
St. Bee's Hd.
Cleator Moor
B5345
Ennerdale Water
Butte
St. Bees
Egremont
LAK
DISTR
Calder Bridge
SCAFE
Beckermet
A595
Wast Water
Sellafield
Gosforth
NATIO
Seascale
Drigg
Irt
PAR
Ravenglass
Esk
Bootle
Pt. of Ayre
Cranstal
A595
BLACK
COMBE
600
A5093
Andreas
Bride
Gri
A9
Ramsey Bay
Whicham
Kirk
Fu
Sulby
Ramsey
Millo
Ballaugh
A3
Maughold
Haverigg
Duddo
Kirk Michael
A14
SNAEFELL
620
Maughold Hd.
A18
A15
B10
15
Dalton-in-Furn
Laxey
BARROW-IN-FURNESS
Peel
A4
St. John's
B22
A2
Vickerstown
Glenmaye
A27
Onchan
I. of Walney
Foxdale
Douglas
SOUTH BARRULE
483
A24
A5
HEYSHAM
Hilpsford P
Bradda Hd.
A36
A3
A26
A25
Colby
Ballasalla
Port Erin
ISLE OF MAN
BELFAST
(April-Sept)
DUBLIN
(April-Sept)
LIVERPOOL
Castletown
Port St. Mary
Langness
Calf of Man

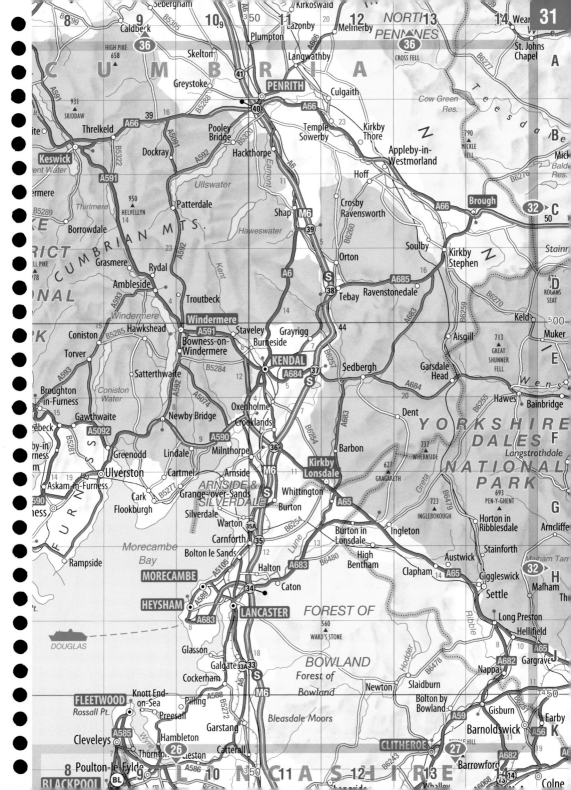

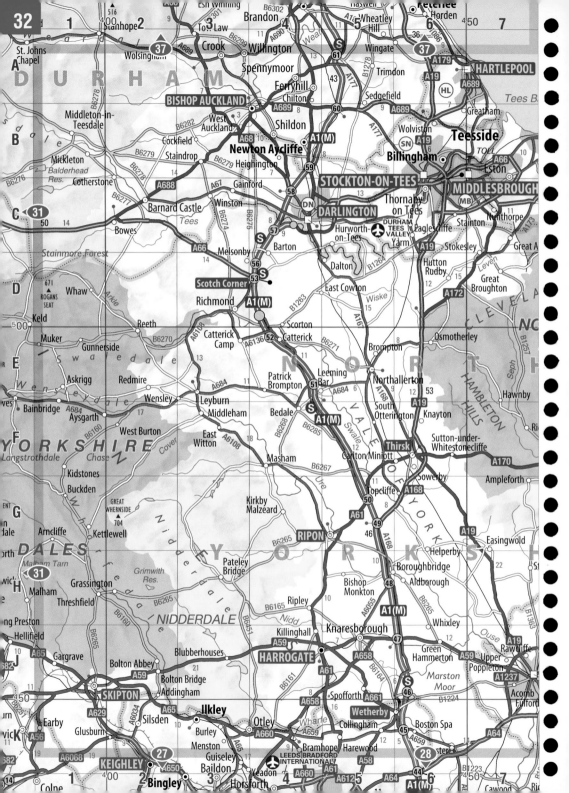

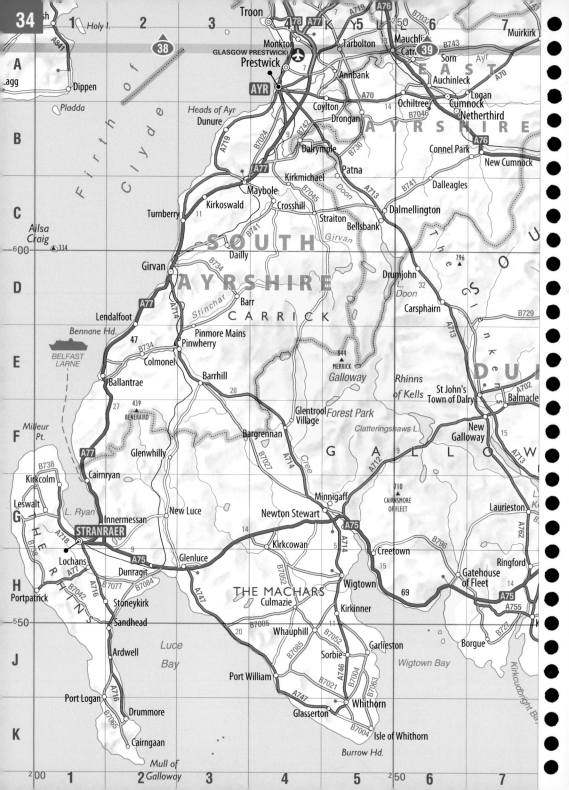

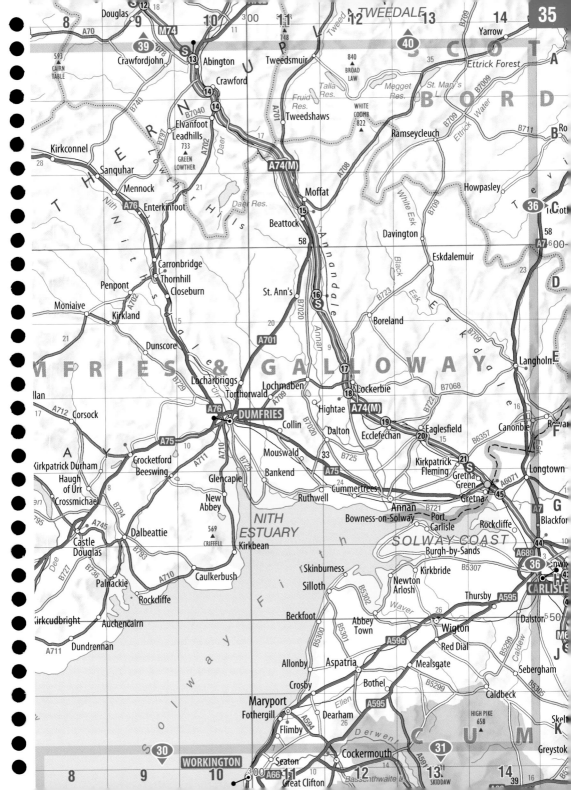

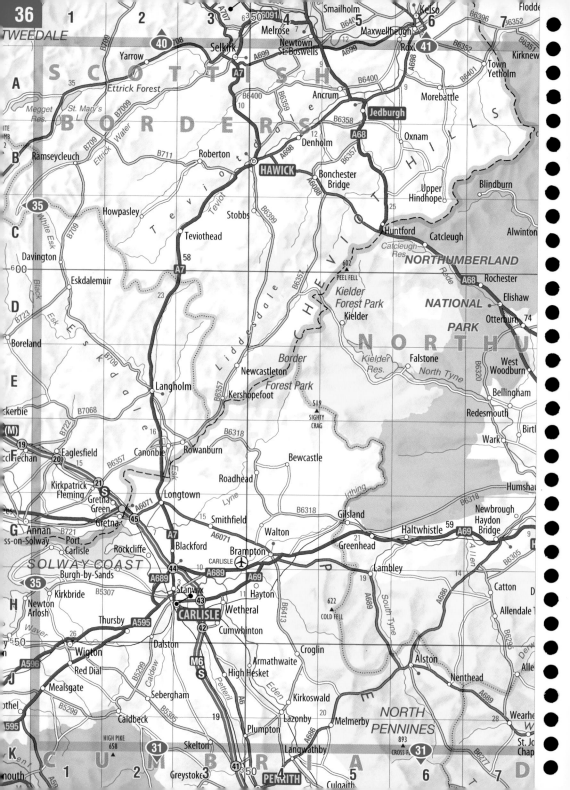

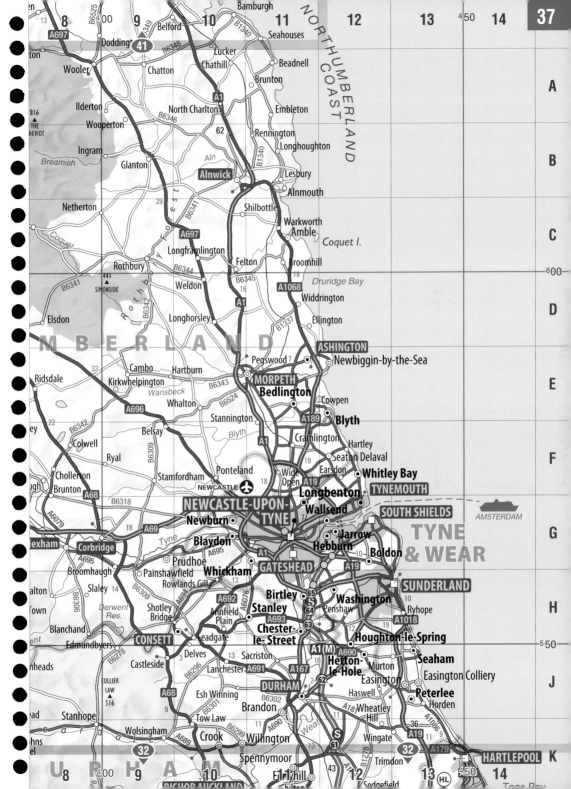

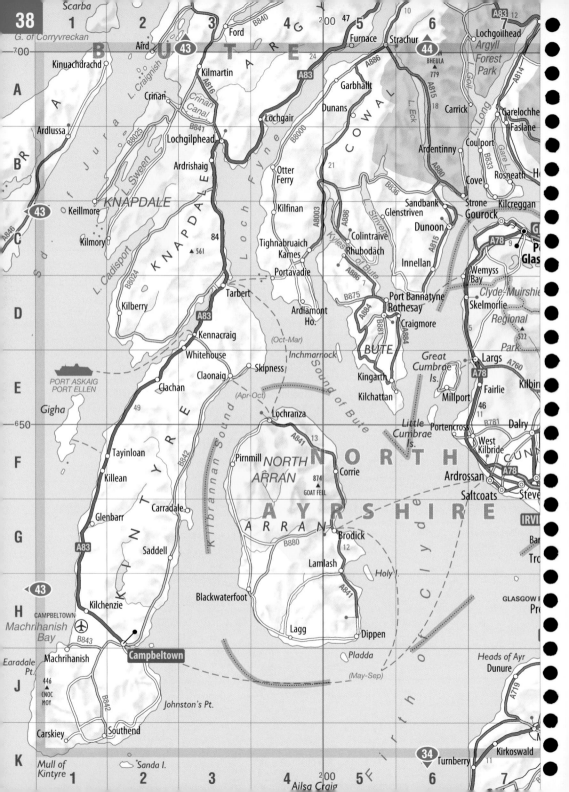

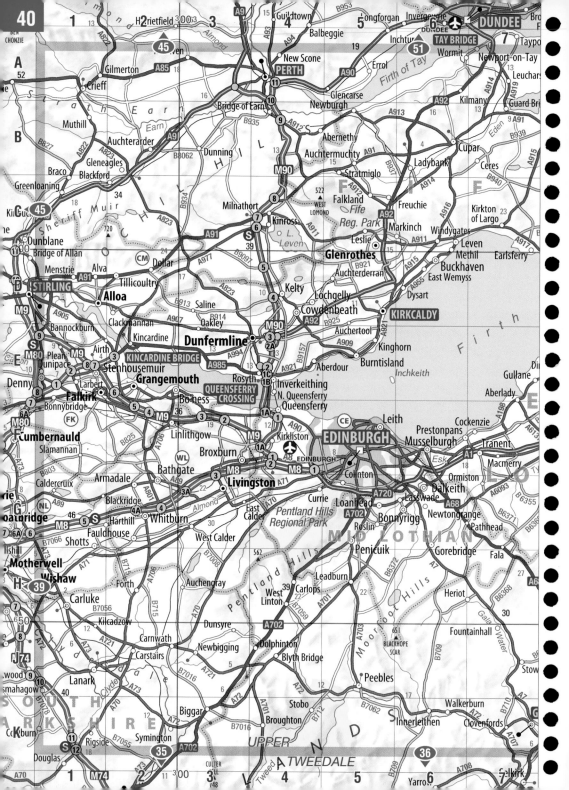

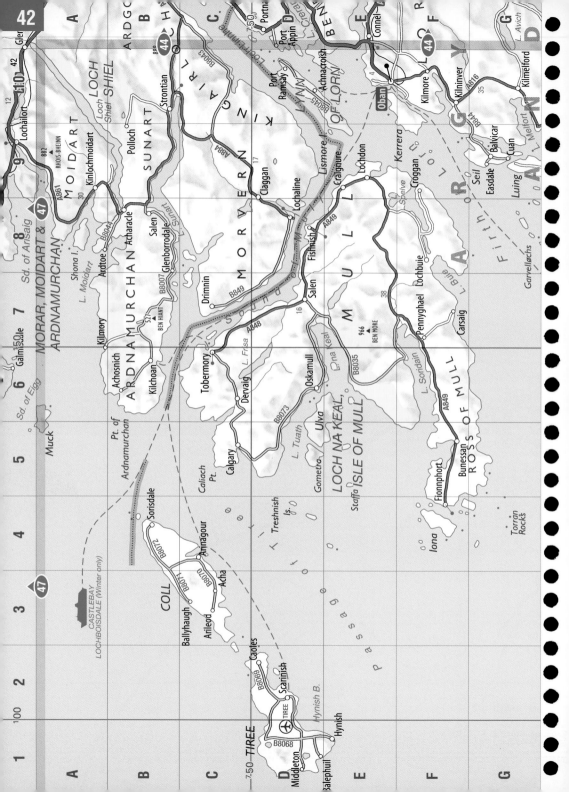

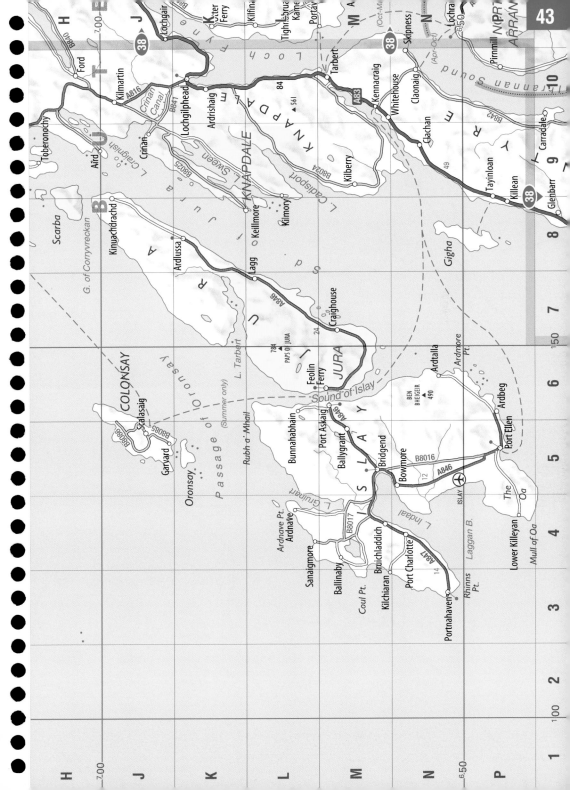

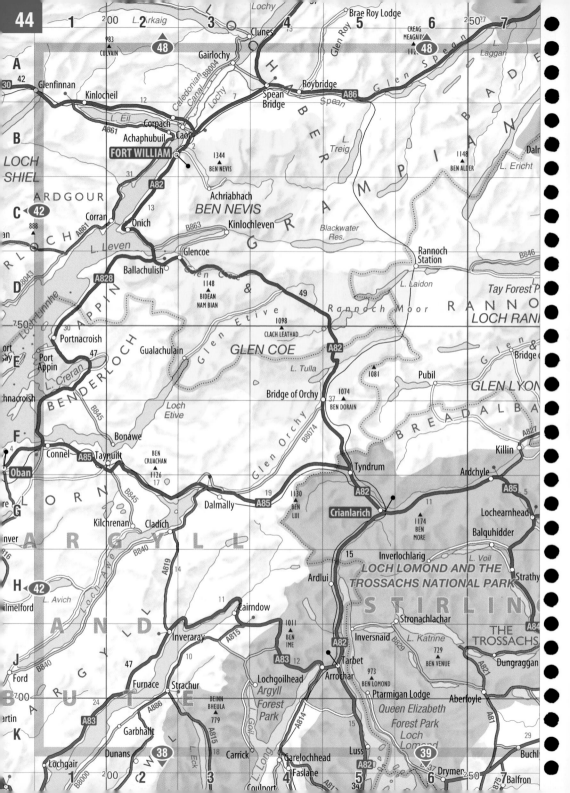

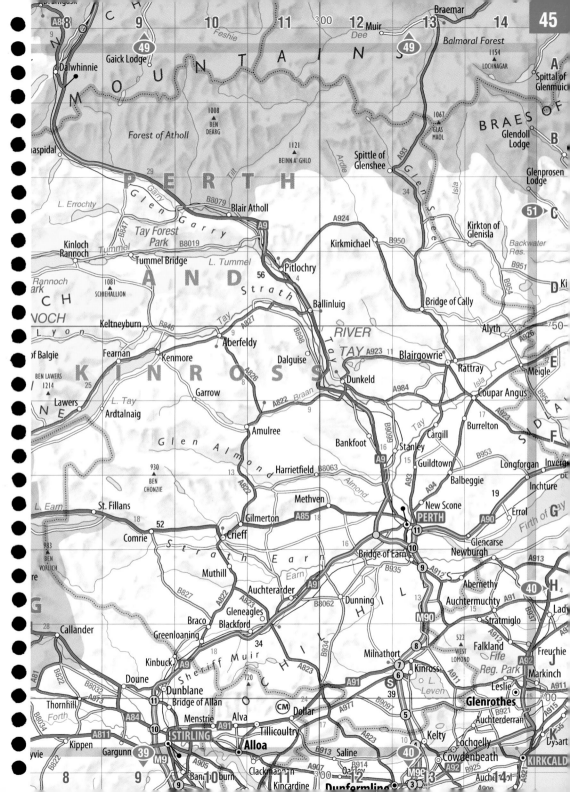

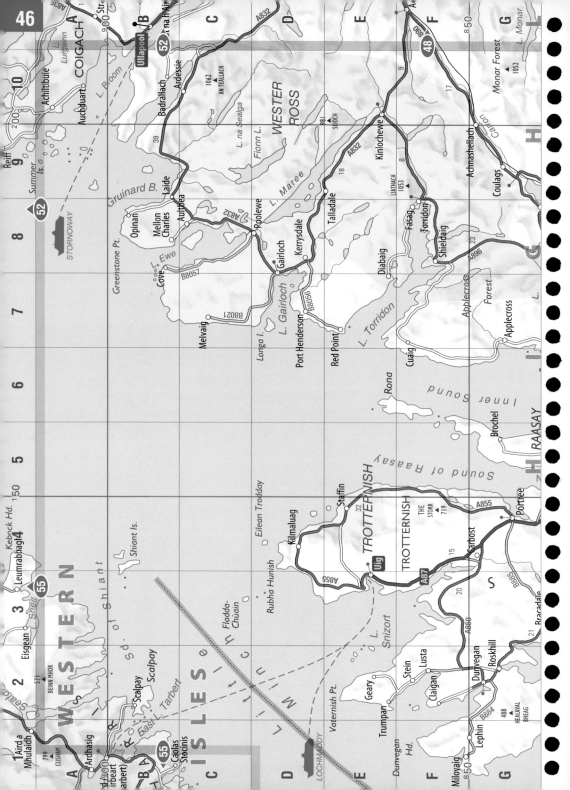

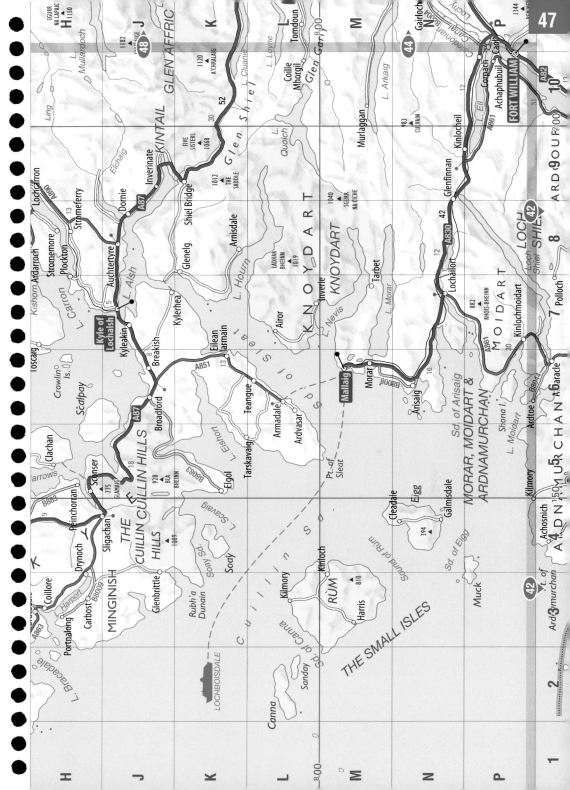

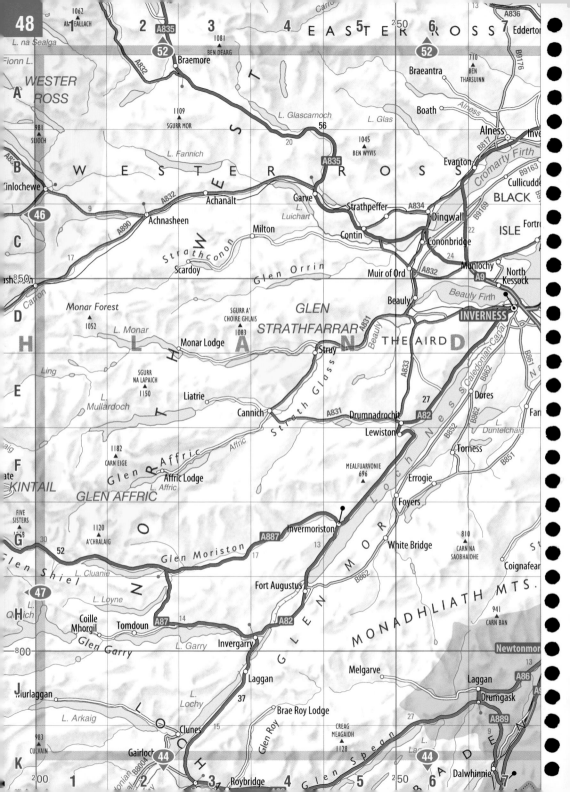

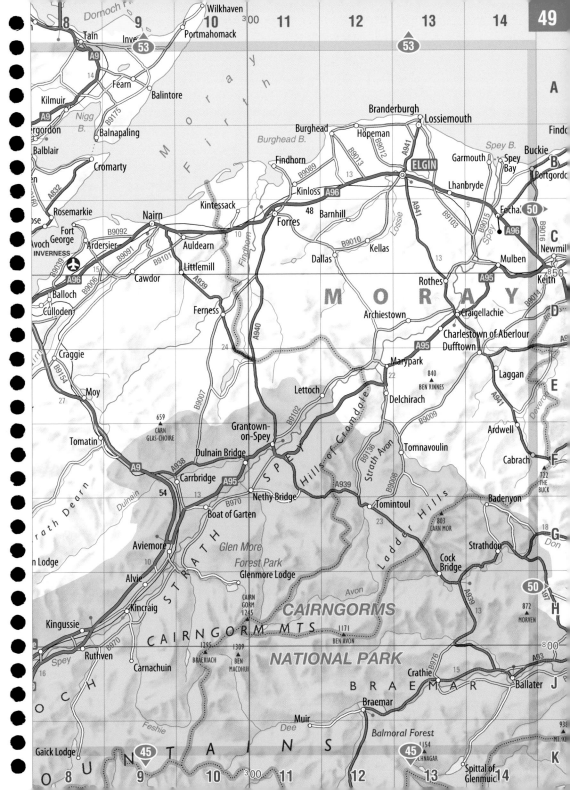

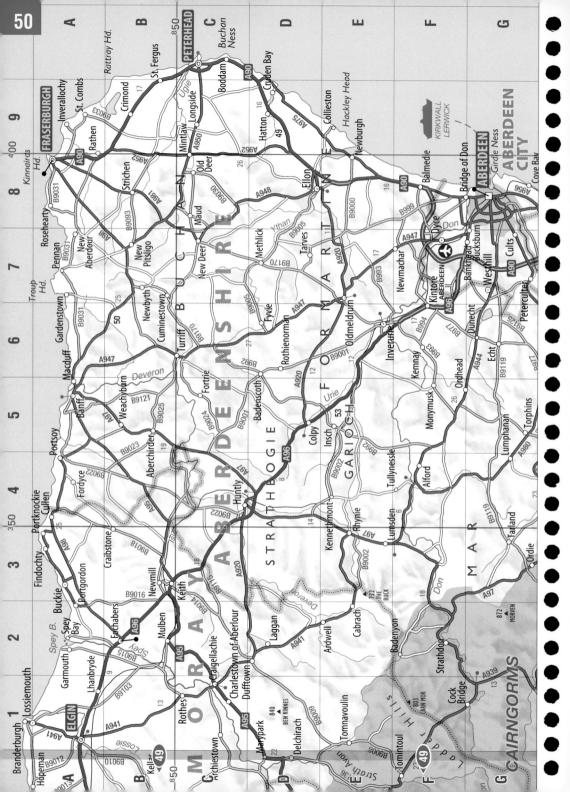

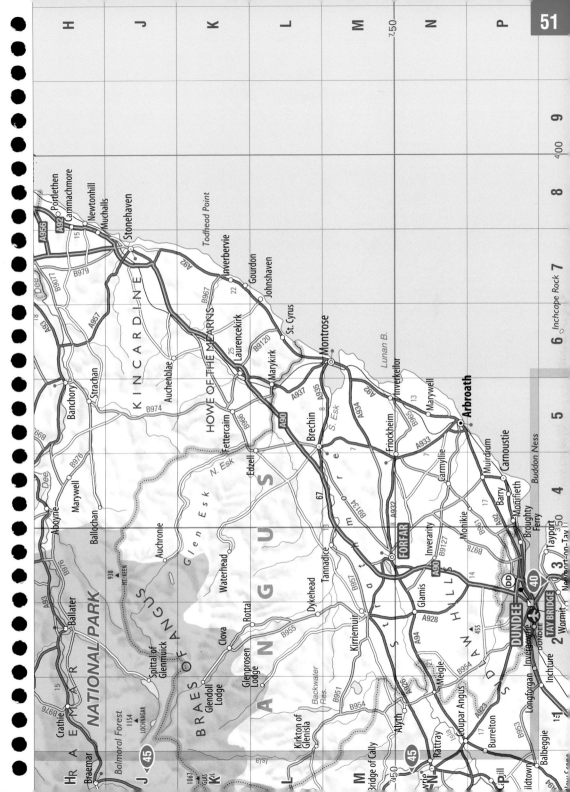

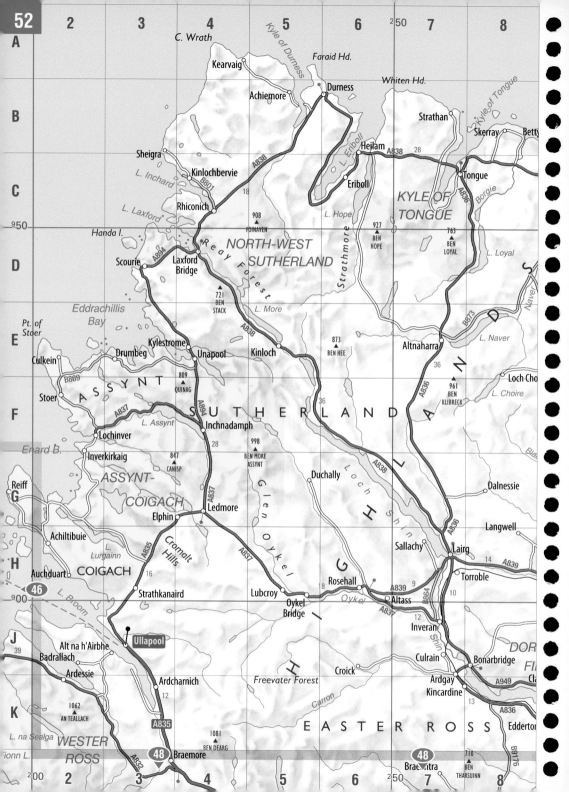

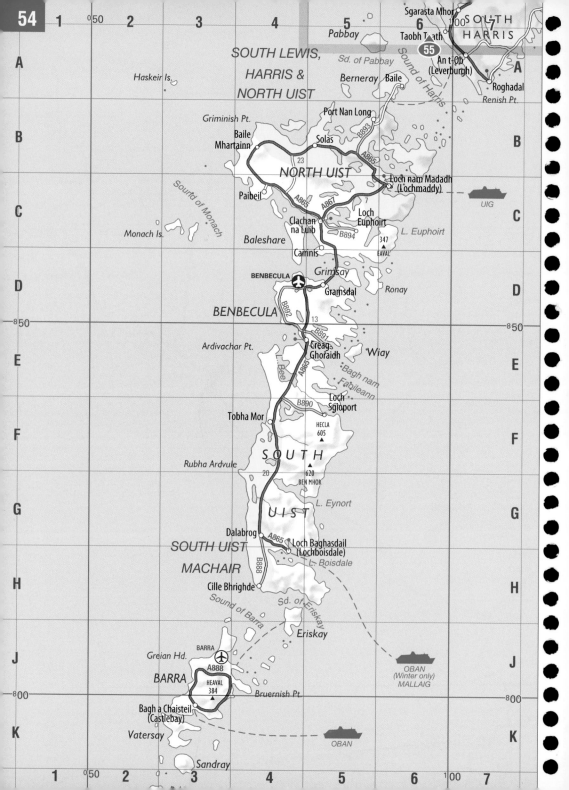

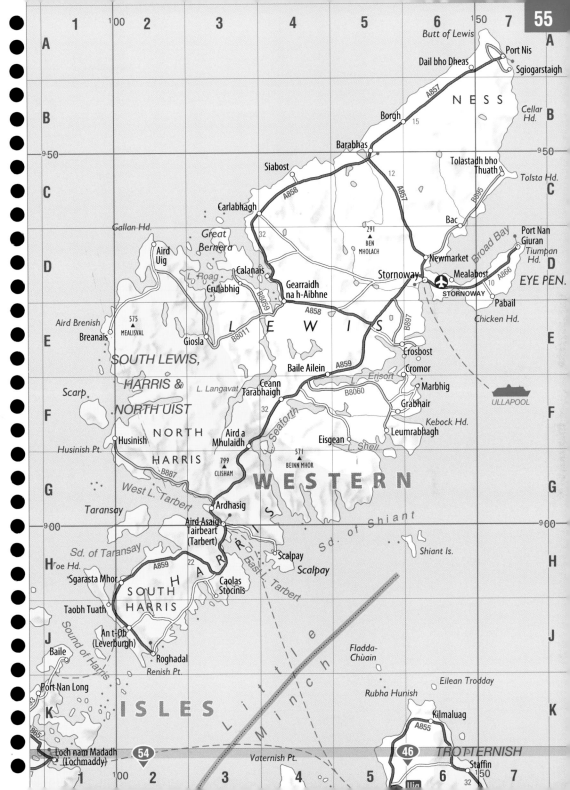

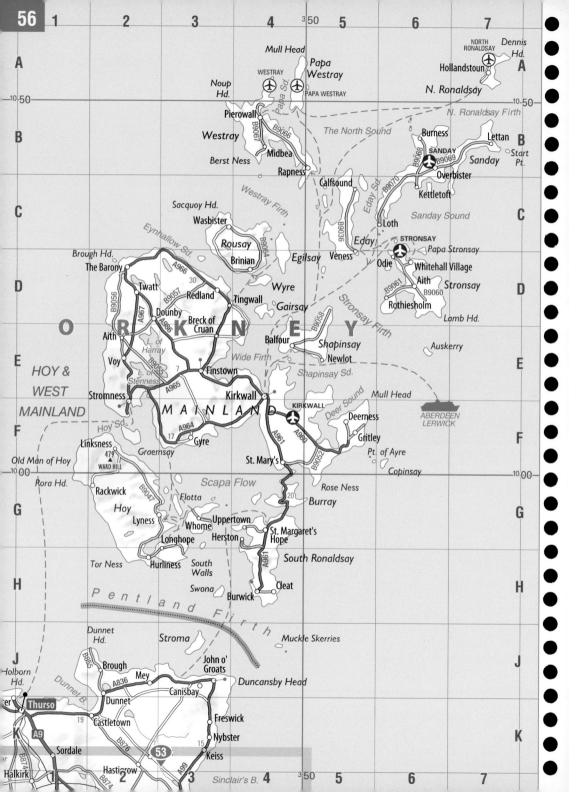

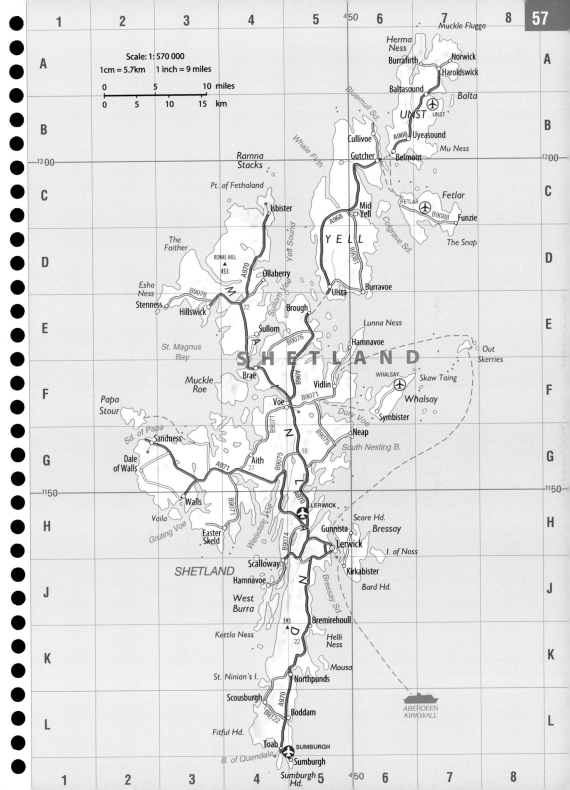

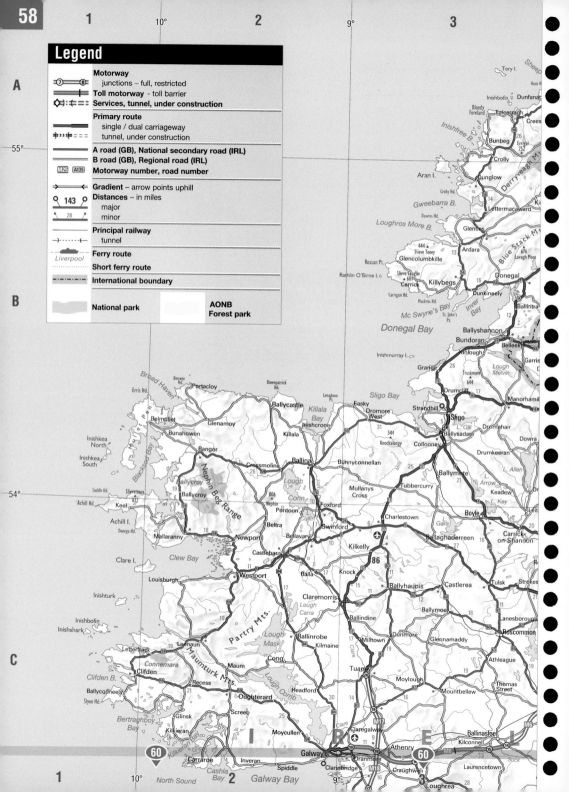

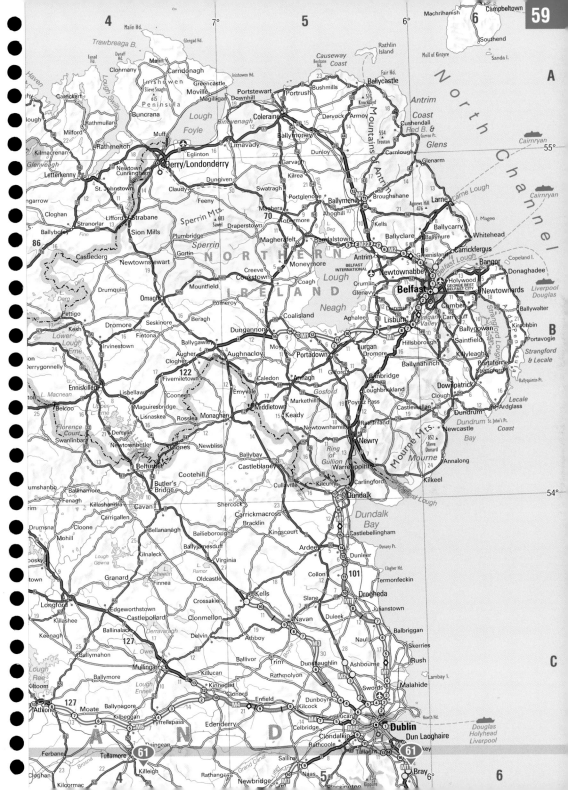

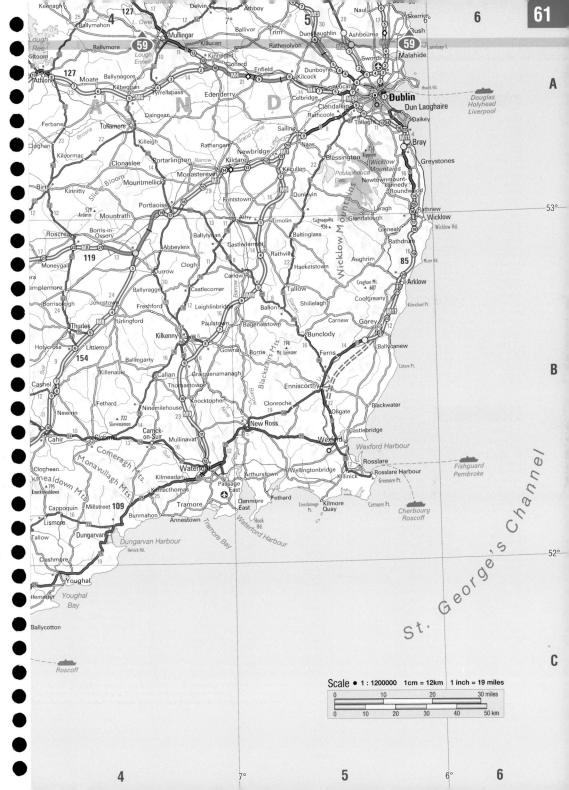

Index to road maps of Ireland

A

Abbey 60 A3
Abbeydorney. 60 B2
Abbeyfeale. 60 B2
Abbeyleix 61 B4
Adare 60 B3
Adrigole 60 C2
Aghalee 59 B5
Ahoghill 59 B5
Allihies 60 C1
Anascaul 60 B1
Annalong 59 B6
Annestown. 61 B4
Antrim. 59 B5
Ardagh 60 B2
Ardara 58 B3
Ardee 59 C5
Ardfert 60 B2
Ardglass 59 B6
Ardgroom 60 C2
Ardkearagh 60 C1
Arklow 61 B5
Armagh. 59 B5
Armoy 59 A5
Arthurstown 61 B5
Ashbourne. 59 C5
Askeaton 60 B3
Athboy 59 C5
Athea 60 B2
Athenry 60 A3
Athleague 58 C3
Athlone 61 A4
Athy 61 B5
Augher 59 B4
Aughnacloy 59 B5
Aughrim 61 B5

B

Bailieborough. 59 C5
Balbriggan 59 C5
Balla 58 C2
Ballaghaderreen 58 C3
Ballina 58 B2
Ballinalack. 59 C4
Ballinamore. 59 B4
Ballinascarty 60 C3
Ballinasloe. 60 A3
Ballindine 58 C3
Ballingarry
  Limerick 60 B3
  Tipperary 61 B4
Ballingeary 60 C2
Ballinhassig. 60 C3
Ballinrobe. 58 C2
Ballinskellings 60 C1
Ballinspittle. 60 C3
Ballintra 58 B3
Ballivor 59 C5
Ballon 61 B5
Ballybay 59 B5
Ballybofey 59 B4
Ballybunion 60 B2
Ballycanew 61 B5
Ballycarry. 59 B6
Ballycastle
  Antrim 59 A5
  Mayo 58 B2
Ballyclare. 59 B6
Ballyconneely 58 C1

Ballycotton 60 C3
Ballycroy 58 B2
Ballydehob 60 C2
Ballyferriter. 60 B1
Ballygawley 59 B4
Ballygowan 59 B6
Ballyhaunis 58 C3
Ballyheige 60 B2
Ballyjamesduff 59 C4
Ballylanders 60 B3
Ballylynan 61 B4
Ballymahon 59 C4
Ballymena 59 B5
Ballymoe 58 C3
Ballymoney 59 A5
Ballymore. 59 C4
Ballymote. 58 B3
Ballynacorra 60 C3
Ballynagore 61 A4
Ballynahinch 59 B6
Ballynure 59 B6
Ballyragget 61 B4
Ballysadare 58 B3
Ballyshannon 58 B3
Ballyvaughan 60 A2
Ballyvourney 60 C2
Ballywalter 59 B6
Baltimore. 60 C2
Baltinglass 61 B5
Banbridge 59 B5
Bandon 60 C3
Bangor
  Down 59 B6
  Mayo 58 B2
Banteer. 60 B3
Bantry 60 C2
Beaufort. 60 B2
Belcoo. 59 B4
Belfast 59 B6
Belgooly 60 C3
Bellananagh 59 C4
Bellavary 58 C2
Belleek 58 B3
Belmullet 58 B2
Beltra 58 C2
Belturbet 59 B4
Beragh 59 B4
Birr 61 A4
Blackwater 61 B5
Blarney 60 C3
Blessington 61 A5
Borris 61 B4
Borris-in-Ossory 61 B4
Borrisokane. 60 B3
Borrisoleigh 61 B4
Boyle 58 C3
Bracklin 59 C5
Bray. 61 A5
Broadford. 60 B3
Broughshane 59 B5
Bruff 60 B3
Bunahowen 58 B2
Bunbeg 58 A3
Bunclody 61 B5
Buncrana 59 A4
Bundoran 58 B3
Bunmahon 61 B4
Bunnyconnellan 58 B2
Bunratty 60 B3
Bushmills 59 A5
Butler's Bridge 59 B4
Buttevant 60 B3

C

Caher 61 B4
Caherciveen 60 C1
Caherdaniel. 60 C1
Caledon 59 B5
Callan 61 B4
Camp. 60 B2
Cappamore 60 B3
Cappoquin 61 B4
Carlingford 59 B5
Carlow 61 B5
Carndonagh 59 A4
Carnew 61 B5
Carnlough 59 B6
Carraroe 60 A2
Carrick 58 B3
Carrickart 59 A4
Carrickfergus 59 B6
Carrickmacross 59 C5
Carrick-on-
  Shannon 58 C3
Carrick-on-Suir. 61 B4
Carrigallen 59 C4
Carryduff 59 B6
Cashel 61 B4
Castlebar 58 C2
Castlebellingham. . . .59 C5
Castleblaney 59 B5
Castlebridge 61 B5
Castlecomer 61 B4
Castlederg 59 B4
Castledermot 61 B5
Castleisland. 60 B2
Castlemaine 60 B2
Castlemartyr 60 C3
Castlepollard. 59 C4
Castlerea 58 C3
Castletown
  Bearhaven. 60 C2
Castletownroche 60 B3
Castlewellan 59 B6
Cavan 59 C4
Celbridge 61 A5
Charlestown 58 C3
Charleville 60 B3
Clarecastle 60 B3
Claregalway 60 A3
Claremorris 58 C3
Clarinbridge 60 A3
Clashmore 61 B4
Claudy 59 B4
Clifden 58 C1
Clogh 61 B4
Cloghan
  Donegal 59 B4
  Offaly 61 A4
Clogheen 61 B4
Clogher 59 B4
Cloghjordan 60 B3
Clonakilty 60 C3
Clonaslee 61 A4
Clondalkin 61 A5
Clones 59 B4
Clonmany 59 A4
Clonmel 61 B4
Clonmellon 59 C4
Clonord 59 C4
Clonroche 61 B5
Cloone 59 C4
Clough 59 B6
Cloyne 60 C3

Coachford 60 C3
Coagh 59 B5
Coalisland 59 B5
Cóbh 60 C3
Coleraine 59 A5
Collon 59 C5
Collooney. 58 B3
Comber 59 B6
Cong 58 C2
Conna 60 B3
Connaugh 60 B3
Cookstown. 59 B5
Coolgreany 61 B5
Cooneen 59 B4
Cootehill 59 B4
Cork. 60 C3
Craughwell 60 A3
Creeslough 59 A4
Creeve. 59 B5
Crolly. 58 A3
Crookhaven 60 C2
Crookstown 60 C3
Croom 60 B3
Crossakiel 59 C4
Crosshaven 60 C3
Crossmolina 58 B2
Crumlin 59 B5
Crusheen 60 B3
Cullaville 59 B5
Cushendall. 59 A5

D

Daingean 61 A4
Dalkey 61 A5
Darragh 60 B2
Delvin 59 C4
Derrygonnelly 59 B4
Derrylin 59 B4
Derry/Londonderry . .59 B4
Dervock 59 A5
Dingle 60 B1
Donaghadee 59 B6
Donegal 58 B3
Doonbeg 60 B2
Downhill. 59 A5
Downpatrick 59 B6
Dowra 58 B3
Draperstown 59 B5
Drimoleague. 60 C2
Drogheda 59 C5
Dromahair 58 B3
Dromcolliher. 60 B3
Dromore
  Down 59 B5
  Tyrone 59 B4
Dromore West 58 B3
Drumcliff 58 B3
Drumkeeran 58 B3
Drumquin. 59 B4
Drumshanbo 58 B3
Drumsna 59 C4
Dublin 61 A5
Duleek 59 C5
Dunboyne. 59 C5
Dundalk 59 B5
Dundrum 59 B6
Dunfanaghy 59 A4
Dungannon 59 B5
Dungarvan 61 B4
Dungiven 59 B5
Dunglow 58 B3

Dungourney 60 C3
Dunkineely 58 B3
Dun Laoghaire 61 A5
Dunlavin 61 A5
Dunleer 59 C5
Dunloy 59 A5
Dunmanway 60 C2
Dunmore 58 C3
Dunmore East. 61 B5
Dunmurry. 59 B5
Dunshaughlin 59 C5
Durrow 61 B4
Durrus 60 C2

E

Easky. 58 B3
Edenderry 61 A4
Edgeworthstown 59 C4
Eglinton 59 A4
Emyvale 59 B5
Enfield 59 C5
Ennis 60 B3
Enniscorthy 61 B5
Enniskean 60 C3
Enniskillen. 59 B4
Ennistimon 60 B2

F

Falcarragh 58 A3
Farranfore 60 B2
Feeny 59 B4
Fenagh 59 B4
Fenit 60 B2
Ferbane 61 A4
Fermoy 60 B3
Ferns 61 B5
Fethard
  Tipperary 61 B4
  Wexford 61 B5
Finnea 59 C4
Fintona 59 B4
Fivemiletown 59 B4
Fontstown 61 A5
Foxford 58 C2
Foynes 60 B2
Freshford 61 B4

G

Galway 60 A2
Garrison 58 B3
Garvagh 59 B5
Gilford 59 B5
Glenamoy 58 B2
Glenarm 59 B6
Glenavy 59 B5
Glenbeigh 60 B2
Glencolumbkille. 58 B3
Glendalough 61 A5
Glenealy 61 B5
Glengarriff. 60 C2
Glennamaddy 58 C3
Glenties 58 B3
Glin 60 B2
Glinsk 60 A2
Gorey 61 B5
Gort 60 A3
Gortin 59 B4

Gowran 61 B4
Graiguenamanagh . . 61 B5
Granard 59 C4
Grange 58 B3
Greencastle 59 A5
Greenisland 59 B6
Greystones 61 A5

H

Hacketstown 61 B5
Headford 58 C2
Herbertstown 60 B3
Hillsborough 59 B5
Holycross 61 B4
Holywood 59 B6
Hospital 60 B3

I

Inagh 60 B2
Inishannon 60 C3
Inishcrone 58 B2
Inveran 60 A2
Irvinestown 59 B4

J

Johnstown 61 B4
Julianstown 59 C5

K

Kanturk 60 B3
Keadew 58 B3
Keady 59 B5
Keel 58 C1
Keenagh 59 C4
Kells
  Antrim 59 B5
  Meath 59 C5
Kenmare 60 C2
Kesh 59 B4
Kilbaha 60 B2
Kilbeggan 61 A4
Kilcock 59 C5
Kilconnell 60 A3
Kilcormac 61 A4
Kilcullen 61 A5
Kilcurry 59 B5
Kildare 61 A5
Kildorrery 60 B3
Kilgarvan 60 C2
Kilkee 60 B2
Kilkeel 59 B5
Kilkelly 58 C3
Kilkenny 61 B4
Kilkieran 60 A2
Kilkinlea 60 B2
Killadysert 60 B2
Killala 58 B2
Killaloe 60 B3
Killarney 60 B2
Killashandra 59 B4
Killashee 59 C4
Killeigh 61 A4
Killenaule 61 B4
Killimor 60 A3
Killinaboy 60 B2

Killinick 61 B5
Killorglin 60 B2
Killucan 59 C4
Killybegs 58 B3
Killyleagh 59 B6
Kilmacrenan 59 A4
Kilmacthomas 61 B4
Kilmaine 58 C2
Kilmallock 60 B3
Kilmeadan 61 B4
Kilmeedy 60 B3
Kilmore Quay 61 B5
Kilnaleck 59 C4
Kilrea 59 B5
Kilrush 60 B2
Kiltoom 58 C3
Kingarrow 58 B3
Kingscourt 59 C5
Kinlough 58 B3
Kinnegad 59 C4
Kinnitty 61 A4
Kinsale 60 C3
Kinvarra 60 A3
Kircubbin 59 B6
Knock 58 C3
Knocktopher 61 B4

L

Laban 60 A3
Lanesborough 59 C4
Laragh 61 A5
Larne 59 B6
Lauragh 60 C2
Laurencetown 60 A3
Leap 60 C2
Leenaun 58 C2
Leighlinbridge 61 B5
Leitrim 58 C3
Letterfrack 58 C2
Letterkenny 59 B4
Lettermacaward 58 B3
Lifford 59 B4
Limavady 59 A5
Limerick 60 B3
Lisbellaw 59 B4
Lisburn 59 B5
Liscannor 60 B2
Lisdoonvarna 60 A2
Lismore 61 B4
Lisnaskea 59 B4
Lissycasey 60 B2
Listowel 60 B2
Littleton 61 B4
Longford 59 C4
Loughbrickland 59 B5
Loughrea 60 A3
Louisburgh 58 C2
Lucan 61 A5
Lurgan 59 B5

M

Macroom 60 C3
Maghera 59 B5
Magherafelt 59 B5
Magilligan 59 A5
Maguiresbridge 59 B4
Malahide 59 C5
Malin 59 A4
Mallaranny 58 C2

Mallow 60 B3
Manorhamilton 58 B3
Markethill 59 B5
Maum 58 C2
Middletown 59 B5
Midleton 60 C3
Milford 59 A4
Millstreet 60 B3
  Cork 60 B2
Milltown
  Galway 58 C3
  Kerry 60 B1
Milltown Malbay 60 B2
Mitchelstown 60 B3
Moate 61 A4
Mohill 59 C4
Monaghan 59 B5
Monasterevin 61 A4
Moneygall 61 B4
Moneymore 59 B5
Mount Bellew 58 C3
Mountfield 59 B4
Mountmellick 61 A4
Mountrath 61 B4
Moville 59 A4
Moy 59 B5
Moycullen 60 A2
Moylough 58 C3
Muckross 60 B2
Muff 59 A4
Muine Bheag 61 B5
Mullanys Cross 58 B3
Mullinavat 61 B4
Mullingar 59 C4

N

Naas 61 A5
Naul 59 C5
Navan 59 C5
Nenagh 60 B3
Newbliss 59 B4
Newbridge 61 A5
Newcastle 59 B6
Newcastle West 60 B3
Newinn 61 B4
Newmarket 60 B3
Newmarket-on-
  Fergus 60 B3
Newport
  Mayo 58 C2
  Tipperary 60 B3
New Ross 61 B5
Newry 59 B5
Newtownabbey 59 B6
Newtownards 59 B6
Newtownbutler 59 B4
Newtown
  Cunningham 59 B4
Newtownhamilton . . . 59 B5
Newtownmount-
  kennedy 61 A5
Newtown Sands 60 B2
Newtownstewart 59 B4
Ninemilehouse 61 B4

O

Oilgate 61 B5
Oldcastle 59 C4

Omagh 59 B4
Oranmore 60 A3
Oughterard 58 C2

P

Pallas Green 60 B3
Parknasilla 60 C2
Passage East 61 B5
Patrickswell 60 B3
Paulstown 61 B4
Peterswell 60 A3
Pettigo 59 B4
Plumbridge 59 B4
Pomeroy 59 B5
Pontoon 58 C2
Portacloy 58 B2
Portadown 59 B5
Portaferry 59 B6
Portarlington 61 A4
Portavogie 59 B6
Portglenone 59 B5
Portlaoise 61 A4
Portmagne 60 C1
Portroe 60 B3
Portrush 59 A5
Portstewart 59 A5
Portumna 60 A3
Poyntz Pass 59 B5

R

Randalstown 59 B5
Rathangan 61 A5
Rathcoole 61 A5
Rathcormack 60 B3
Rathdrum 61 B5
Rathfriland 59 B5
Rathkeale 60 B3
Rathmelton 59 A4
Rathmolyon 59 C5
Rathmore 60 B2
Rathmullan 59 A4
Rathnew 61 B5
Rathvilly 61 B5
Recess 58 C2
Ringaskiddy 60 C3
Roosky 59 C4
Roscommon 58 C3
Roscrea 61 B4
Rosslare 61 B5
Rosslare Harbour . . . 61 B5
Rosslea 59 B4
Roundwood 61 A5
Rush 59 C5

S

Saintfield 59 B6
Sallins 61 A5
Scarriff 60 B3
Screeb 60 A2
Seskinore 59 B4
Shanagolden 60 B2
Shercock 59 C5
Shillelagh 61 B5
Silvermines 60 B3
Sion Mills 59 B4
Skerries 59 C5
Skibbereen 60 C2

Slane 59 C5
Sligo 58 B3
Sneem 60 C2
Spiddle 60 A2
St. Johnstown 59 B4
Strabane 59 B4
Stradbally 60 B1
Strandhill 58 B3
Strangford 59 B6
Stranorlar 59 B4
Strokestown 58 C3
Swanlinbar 59 B4
Swatragh 59 B5
Swinford 58 C3
Swords 59 C5

T

Tallaght 61 A5
Tallow 60 B3
Tarbert 60 B2
Templederry 60 B3
Templemore 61 B4
Termonfeckin 59 C5
Thomas Street 58 C3
Thomastown 61 B4
Thurles 61 B4
Timoleague 60 C3
Timolin 61 B5
Tipperary 60 B3
Tobermore 59 B5
Toomyvara 60 B3
Toormore 60 C2
Tralee 60 B2
Tramore 61 B4
Trim 59 C5
Tuam 58 C3
Tubbercory 58 B3
Tulla 60 B3
Tullamore 61 A4
Tullow 61 B5
Tulsk 58 C3
Tyrrellspass 61 A4

U

Urlingford 61 B4

V

Virginia 59 C4

W

Warrenpoint 59 B5
Waterford 61 B4
Watergrasshill 60 B3
Waterville 60 C1
Wellingtonbridge . . . 61 B5
Westport 58 C2
Wexford 61 B5
Whitegate 60 C3
Whitehead 59 B6
Wicklow 61 B5

Y

Youghal 61 C4

Index to road maps of Great Britain

How to use the index

Example

Gillingham Dorset **5** A11

— grid square

— page number

— county or unitary authority (only shown for duplicate names)

Abbreviations used in the index

Aberdeen **Aberdeen City**	Glasgow **City of Glasgow**	Poole **Poole**
Aberds **Aberdeenshire**	Glos **Gloucestershire**	Powys **Powys**
Ald **Alderney**	Gtr Man **Greater Manchester**	Ptsmth **Portsmouth**
Anglesey **Isle of Anglesey**	Guern **Guernsey**	Reading **Reading**
Angus **Angus**	Gwyn **Gwynedd**	Redcar **Redcar and Cleveland**
Argyll **Argyll and Bute**	Halton **Halton**	Renfs **Renfrewshire**
Bath **Bath and North East Somerset**	Hants **Hampshire**	Rhondda **Rhondda Cynon Taff**
Bedford **Bedford**	Hereford **Herefordshire**	Rutland **Rutland**
Bl Gwent **Blaenau Gwent**	Herts **Hertfordshire**	S Ayrs **South Ayrshire**
Blackburn **Blackburn with Darwen**	Highld **Highland**	S Glos **South Gloucestershire**
Blackpool **Blackpool**	Hrtlpl **Hartlepool**	S Lanark **South Lanarkshire**
Bmouth **Bournemouth**	Hull **Hull**	S Yorks **South Yorkshire**
Borders **Scottish Borders**	IoM **Isle of Man**	Scilly **Scilly**
Brack **Bracknell**	IoW **Isle of Wight**	Shetland **Shetland**
Bridgend **Bridgend**	Invclyd **Inverclyde**	Shrops **Shropshire**
Brighton **City of Brighton and Hove**	Jersey **Jersey**	Slough **Slough**
Bristol **City and County of Bristol**	Kent **Kent**	Som **Somerset**
Bucks **Buckinghamshire**	Lancs **Lancashire**	Soton **Southampton**
C Beds **Central Bedfordshire**	Leicester **City of Leicester**	Staffs **Staffordshire**
Caerph **Caerphilly**	Leics **Leicestershire**	Southend **Southend-on-Sea**
Cambs **Cambridgeshire**	Lincs **Lincolnshire**	Stirling **Stirling**
Cardiff **Cardiff**	London **Greater London**	Stockton **Stockton-on-Tees**
Carms **Carmarthenshire**	Luton **Luton**	Stoke **Stoke-on-Trent**
Ceredig **Ceredigion**	M Keynes **Milton Keynes**	Suff **Suffolk**
Ches E **Cheshire East**	M Tydf **Merthyr Tydfil**	Sur **Surrey**
Ches W **Cheshire West and Chester**	Mbro **Middlesbrough**	Swansea **Swansea**
Clack **Clackmannanshire**	Medway **Medway**	Swindon **Swindon**
Conwy **Conwy**	Mers **Merseyside**	T&W **Tyne and Wear**
Corn **Cornwall**	Midloth **Midlothian**	Telford **Telford and Wrekin**
Cumb **Cumbria**	Mon **Monmouthshire**	Thurrock **Thurrock**
Darl **Darlington**	Moray **Moray**	Torbay **Torbay**
Denb **Denbighshire**	N Ayrs **North Ayrshire**	Torf **Torfaen**
Derby **City of Derby**	N Lincs **North Lincolnshire**	V Glam **The Vale of Glamorgan**
Derbys **Derbyshire**	N Lanark **North Lanarkshire**	W Berks **West Berkshire**
Devon **Devon**	N Som **North Somerset**	W Dunb **West Dunbartonshire**
Dorset **Dorset**	N Yorks **North Yorkshire**	W Isles **Western Isles**
Dumfries **Dumfries and Galloway**	NE Lincs **North East Lincolnshire**	W Loth **West Lothian**
Dundee **Dundee City**	Neath **Neath Port Talbot**	W Mid **West Midlands**
Durham **Durham**	Newport **City and County of Newport**	W Sus **West Sussex**
E Ayrs **East Ayrshire**	Norf **Norfolk**	W Yorks **West Yorkshire**
E Dunb **East Dunbartonshire**	Northants **Northamptonshire**	Warks **Warwickshire**
E Loth **East Lothian**	Northumb **Northumberland**	Warr **Warrington**
E Renf **East Renfrewshire**	Nottingham **City of Nottingham**	Wilts **Wiltshire**
E Sus **East Sussex**	Notts **Nottinghamshire**	Windsor **Windsor and Maidenhead**
E Yorks **East Riding of Yorkshire**	Orkney **Orkney**	Wokingham **Wokingham**
Edin **City of Edinburgh**	Oxon **Oxfordshire**	Worcs **Worcestershire**
Essex **Essex**	Pboro **Peterborough**	Wrex **Wrexham**
Falk **Falkirk**	Pembs **Pembrokeshire**	York **City of York**
Fife **Fife**	Perth **Perth and Kinross**	
Flint **Flintshire**	Plym **Plymouth**	

Fairlight 11 H9
Fakenham 24 B4
Fala 40 G7
Faldingworth 29 F9
Falkirk 39 B13
Falkland 40 C5
Falmer 10 J4
Falmouth 2 H6
Falstone 36 E6
Fareham 9 G10
Faringdon 15 G11
Farnborough
Hants 9 B13
W Berks 15 H13
Farndon 20 A5
Farnham 9 C13
Farnworth 27 E8
Farr 48 E7
Fasag 46 F9
Faslane 38 A7
Fauldhouse 40 G2
Faversham 11 C11
Fawley 9 G9
Fazeley 21 F13
Fearn 49 A9
Fearnan 45 E9
Feckenham 21 K11
Felixstowe 25 M8
Felton 37 C10
Feltwell 24 F2
Fenny Bentley 21 A12
Fenny Compton 15 A13
Fenny Stratford 16 B3
Fenwick 39 F9
Feock 2 H6
Feolin Ferry 43 M6
Ferndown 8 H5
Ferness 49 D10
Fernhurst 9 E14
Ferryhill 32 A4
Ferryside 12 F7
Fettercairn 51 K5
Filby 24 D9
Filey 33 F13
Fillongley 21 H13
Filton 14 J5
Fincham 24 E1
Finchingfield 17 B11
Finchley 16 F7
Findhorn 49 B11
Findochty 50 A3
Findon 10 J2
Finedon 23 H8
Finningley 28 E5
Finstown 56 E3
Fintry 39 B11
Fionnphort 42 F4
Fishbourne 9 H10
Fishguard 12 C3
Fishnish 42 D8
Fishtoft 23 A12
Flamborough 33 G14
Fleet 9 B13
Fleetwood 31 K9
Flimby 35 K11
Flint 26 H3
Flitwick 16 B5
Flodden 41 K12
Flookburgh 31 G9
Fochabers 50 B2
Foel 19 J10
Folkestone 11 F13
Folkingham 23 B9
Fontmell Magna 8 F3
Ford 43 H10
Forden 20 F3
Fordham 25 H1
Fordingbridge 8 F6
Fordyce 50 A4
Forest Row 10 F5
Forfar 51 M3
Formby 26 E3
Forres 49 C11
Forsinain 53 D11
Forsinard 53 D10
Fort Augustus 48 H4
Fort George
Highland 49 C8
Jersey 4 Jersey
Forth 40 H2
Forth Road Bridge 40 E4
Fortrie 50 C5
Fortrose 49 C8
Fortuneswell 5 F10
Fort William 44 B3
Fothergill 35 K11
Fotheringhay 23 F9
Foulden 41 H12
Foulsham 24 C5
Fountainhall 40 J7
Four Lanes 2 H4
Fovant 8 E5
Fowey 3 F9
Fownhope 14 C4
Foxdale 30 H2
Foyers 48 F6
Fraddon 2 F6
Framlingham 25 J7
Frampton on Severn 14 F6
Frant 10 F6
Fraserburgh 50 A8
Freckleton 26 C5
Freethorpe 24 E9
Fremington 6 H4
Frensham 9 C13
Freshwater 9 J8
Freshwater East 12 G4
Fressingfield 24 H7
Freswick 53 B15
Freuchie 40 C5
Friday Bridge 23 E13
Fridaythorpe 33 H10
Frimley 9 B13
Frinton-on-Sea 25 P7
Friockheim 51 M4
Frizington 30 C6
Frodsham 26 H6
Frome 8 C2
Frongoch 18 G9
Froxfield 15 K11
Fulbourn 23 K14
Fulford 33 K8
Fulwood 26 B6
Funzie 57 C7
Furnace 44 J2
Fyfield 17 E10
Fyvie 50 D6

G

Gaerwen 18 C4
Gaick Lodge 49 K8
Gailey 21 E10
Gainford 32 C3
Gainsborough 28 F7
Gairloch 46 D8
Gairlochy 44 A3
Galashiels 40 K7
Galgate 31 J10
Galmisdale 47 N4
Galmpton 4 H2
Galston 39 G10
Gamlingay 23 K11
Garbhallt 38 A5
Garboldisham 24 G5
Gardenstown 50 A7
Garelochhead 38 A7
Garforth 28 A3
Gargrave 32 J1
Gargunnock 39 A12
Garlieston 34 J5
Garmouth 50 A2
Garrow 45 E10
Garsdale Head 31 E13
Garstang 31 K10
Garston 26 G4
Garton-on-the-
Wolds 33 H11
Garvald 41 F8
Garvard 43 J5
Garve 48 B4
Gatehouse of Fleet 34 H6
Gateshead 37 G11
Gatley 27 G9
Gatwick Airport 10 E3
Gawthwaite 31 F8
Gaydon 15 A12
Gayton 24 D2
Gaywood 24 C1
Gearraidh na h-
Aibhne 55 D4
Geary 46 E2
Geddington 22 G7
Gedney 23 C13
Gedney Drove End 23 C13
Georgeham 6 H3
Gerrards Cross 16 G5
Gifford 41 G8
Giggleswick 31 H14
Gillingham
Dorset 5 A11
Medway 17 J12
Gilmerton 45 G10
Gilsland 36 G5
Gilwern 14 E1
Giosla 55 E3
Girton 23 J13
Girvan 34 D3
Gisburn 31 K14
Gladestry 14 A1
Glamis 51 N2
Glanaman 13 E10
Glanton 37 B9
Glasbury 13 C15
Glasgow 39 D10
Glasserton 34 K5
Glasson 31 J10
Glastonbury 7 H14
Glemsford 25 L3
Glenbarr 38 G1
Glenborrodale 42 B8
Glenbrittle 47 J4
Glencaple 35 G10
Glencarse 45 G14
Glencoe 44 D3
Glendoll Lodge 51 K1
Gleneagles 45 H11
Glenelg 47 K8
Glenfinnan 47 N9
Glenluce 34 H3
Glenmaye 30 G2
Glenmore Lodge 49 H10
Glenprosen Lodge 51 L1
Glenrothes 40 C5
Glenstriven 38 C5
Glentrool Village 34 F4
Glenwhilly 34 F3
Glinton 23 E10
Glossop 27 F11
Gloucester 14 E7
Glusburn 27 A11
Glutt Lodge 53 E11
Glyn Ceiriog 20 C3
Glyncorrwg 13 G12
Glynde 10 J5
Glyndyfrdwy 20 B2
Glyn Neath 13 F12
Gnosall 21 D9
Goathland 33 D10
Gobowen 20 C4
Godalming 9 C14
Godmanchester 23 H11
Godshill 9 J10
Godstone 10 E4
Goldhanger 25 Q4
Golspie 53 J10
Goodrich 14 E4
Goodwick 12 C3
Goole 28 B6
Goonhavern 2 F5
Gordon 41 J9
Gorebridge 40 G6
Gorey 5 Jersey
Goring 16 G1
Goring-by-Sea 10 J2
Gorleston-on-Sea 24 E10
Gorran Haven 3 H8
Gorseinon 13 G9
Gorslas 13 E9
Gosberton 23 B11
Gosfield 25 N2
Gosforth 30 D6
Gosport 9 H11
Goswick 41 J13
Gotham 22 C4
Goudhurst 11 F8
Gourdon 51 K7
Gourock 38 C7
Gowerton 13 G9
Grabhair 55 F5
Grain 11 B9
Grainthorpe 29 E12
Grampound 2 G7
Gramsdal 54 D5
Grangemouth 40 E2
Grange-over-
Sands 31 G10
Grantham 23 B8
Grantown-on-Spey 49 F11
Grantshouse 41 G11
Grasby 29 D9
Grasmere 31 D9
Grassington 32 H2
Grateley 8 C7
Gravesend 17 H11
Grayrigg 31 E11
Grays 17 H11
Grayshott 9 D13
Great Ayton 32 C7
Great Baddow 17 E12
Great Barford 23 K10
Great Bentley 25 N6
Great Bridgeford 21 D9
Great Broughton 32 D7
Great Chesterford 17 A10
Great Clifton 30 B6
Great Dunmow 17 C11
Great Ellingham 24 F5
Great Gidding 23 G10
Greatham 32 B6
Great Harwood 27 B8
Great Horwood 16 B2
Great Malvern 14 B6
Great Massingham 24 C2
Great Missenden 16 E4
Great Oakley 25 N7
Great Sampford 17 B11
Great Shefford 15 J12
Great Shelford 23 K13
Great Somerford 15 H8
Great Staunton 23 H10
Great Torrington 6 K3
Great Wakering 17 G14
Great Waltham 17 D12
Great Witley 21 K8
Great Yarmouth 24 E10
Green Hammerton 32 J6
Greenhead 36 G5
Greenholm 39 G10
Greenlaw 41 J10
Greenloaning 45 J10
Greenock 38 C7
Greenodd 31 F9
Greenway 12 D4
Greenwich 10 B4
Gretna 36 G2
Gretna Green 36 G2
Gretton 23 F8
Greystoke 31 A10
Grimsby 29 D11
Gritley 56 F5
Grizebeck 31 F8
Groby 22 E4
Grove 15 G13
Grundisburgh 25 L7
Gualachulain 44 E3
Guard Bridge 40 B7
Guestling Green 11 H9
Guildford 10 E1
Guildtown 45 F13
Guilsfield 20 E3
Guisborough 33 C8
Guiseley 27 A12
Gullane 40 E7
Gunnerside 32 E1
Gunnislake 3 D12
Gunnista 57 H6
Gutcher 57 B6
Gwalchmai 18 C3
Gwaun-Cae-
Gurwen 13 E10
Gwbert 12 B5
Gweek 2 J4
Gwennap 2 H5
Gwyddelwern 18 F10
Gwytherin 18 D8
Gyre 56 F3

H

Hackney 10 A4
Hackthorpe 31 B11
Haddenham
Bucks 16 E2
Cambs 23 H13
Haddington 41 F8
Haddiscoe 24 F9
Hadleigh
Essex 17 G13
Suff. 25 L5
Hadlow 10 E7
Hadnall 20 D6
Hagworthingham 29 H12
Hailsham 10 J6
Hainton 29 F10
Halberton 4 B4
Halesowen 21 H10
Halesworth 24 H8
Halford 15 B11
Halifax 27 C11
Halkirk 53 C13
Halland 10 H6
Hallow 14 A7
Hallworthy 3 C9
Halstead 25 M3
Halton 31 H11
Haltwhistle 36 G6
Halwill Junction 3 B12
Hambledon 9 F11
Hamble-le-Rice 9 G9
Hambleton
Lancs 26 A4
N Yorks 28 A4
Hamerton 23 H10
Hamilton 39 E12
Hammersmith &
Fulham 10 B3
Hamnavoe
Shetland 57 E6
Shetland 57 J4
Hampstead Norreys 15 J14
Hampton in Arden 21 H13
Hamstreet 11 F11
Handcross 10 G3
Hannington 9 B10
Harbury 22 J2
Harby 22 B6
Hardingstone 22 K6
Harewood 27 A14
Haringey 10 A4
Harlech 18 G5
Harleston 24 G7
Harlow 17 E9
Haroldswick 57 A7
Harpenden 16 D6
Harrietfield 45 F11
Harrietsham 11 D9
Harrington 30 B5
Harris 47 M3
Harrogate 32 J4
Harrold 23 K8
Harrow 16 G6
Harston 23 K13
Hartburn 37 E9
Hartest 25 K3
Hartfield 10 F5
Harthill 40 G2
Hartington 27 J12
Hartland 6 J1
Hartlebury 21 J9
Hartlepool 32 A7
Hartley
Kent 17 J11
Northumb 37 F12
Hartley Wintney 9 B12
Hartpury 14 D6
Hartshill 22 F2
Harvington 15 B9
Harwell 15 H13
Harwich 25 M7

Harworth 28 E5
Haselbury Plucknett 5 C8
Haslemere 9 D13
Haslingden 27 C8
Hassocks 10 H4
Hastigrow 53 C14
Hastings 11 J9
Haswell 37 J12
Hatch Beauchamp 4 B7
Hatfield
Herts 16 E7
S Yorks 28 D5
Hatfield Heath 17 D10
Hatfield Peverel 17 D13
Hatherleigh 3 A13
Hathersage 27 G13
Hatton
Aberds 50 D9
Derbys 21 C13
Haughley 25 J5
Haugh of Urr 35 G8
Haughton 21 D9
Havant 9 G12
Haverfordwest 12 E3
Haverhill 17 A11
Haverigg 30 F7
Havering 17 G10
Hawarden 26 J4
Hawes 31 E14
Hawick 36 B4
Hawkchurch 4 D7
Hawkesbury Upton 14 H6
Hawkhurst 11 G8
Hawkinge 11 F13
Hawkshead 31 E9
Hawnby 32 E7
Haworth 27 B11
Hawsker 33 D11
Haxby 33 J8
Haxey 28 D6
Haydon Bridge 36 G7
Hayfield 27 G11
Hayle 2 H3
Hay-on-Wye 14 B1
Hayton
Cumb 36 H4
E Yorks 33 K10
Haywards Heath 10 G4
Hazel Grove 27 G10
Hazlemere 16 F4
Heacham 24 B1
Headcorn 11 E9
Headley 9 D13
Heanor 22 A3
Heath End 9 A10
Heathfield 10 H6
Heathrow Airport 16 H5
Hebburn 37 G12
Hebden Bridge 27 C10
Heckington 23 A10
Hedge End 9 F10
Hednesford 21 E11
Hedon 29 B10
Heighington 32 B4
Heilam 52 B6
Helensburgh 39 B8
Hellifield 31 J14
Helmsdale 53 G12
Helmsley 33 F8
Helperby 32 G6
Helpringham 23 A10
Helsby 26 H5
Helston 2 J4
Hemel Hempstead 16 E5
Hemingbrough 28 A5
Hempnall 24 F7
Hempton 24 C4
Hemsby 24 D9
Hemsworth 28 C3
Hemyock 4 B5
Henfield 10 H3
Hengoed 7 B10
Henley-in-Arden 21 K12
Henley-on-Thames 16 G2
Henllan 18 D10
Henlow 16 B6
Henstridge 5 B11
Herbrandston 12 F2
Hereford 14 C4
Heriot 40 H7
Hermitage 15 J14
Herne Bay 11 C12
Herstmonceux 10 H7
Herston 56 G4
Hertford 17 D8
Hessle 29 B9
Heswall 26 G3
Hethersett 24 E6
Hetton-le-Hole 37 J12
Hexham 37 G8
Heybridge 17 E13
Heysham 31 H10
Heytesbury 8 C4
Heywood 27 D9
Hibaldstow 29 D8
Higham 17 H12
Higham Ferrers 23 J8
High Bentham 31 G12
High Bickington 6 K4
Highbridge 7 G12
Highclere 9 B9
High Ercall 20 E7
High Hesket 36 J3
High Legh 27 G8
Highley 21 H8
Hightae 35 F11
Highworth 15 G11
High Wycombe 16 F3
Hilborough 24 E3
Hildenborough 10 E6
Hilgay 24 F1
Hillingdon 16 G5
Hillington 24 C2
Hillswick 57 E3
Hilmarton 15 J9
Hilton 21 C13
Hinckley 22 F3
Hinderwell 33 C10
Hindhead 9 D13
Hindley 26 E7
Hindon 8 D4
Hingham 24 E5
Hinstock 20 D8
Hirwaun 13 F13
Histon 23 J13
Hitchin 16 B6
Hockley 17 F13
Hockliffe 16 C4
Hoddesdon 17 E8
Hodnet 20 D7
Hoff 31 C12
Holbeach 23 C12
Holbeach Drove 23 D12
Holbrook 25 M6
Holford 7 G10
Holkham 24 A3
Holland-on-Sea 25 P7
Hollandstoun 56 A7
Hollym 29 B12
Holme-on-Spalding-moor 28 A7
Holmer 14 B4
Holmes Chapel 27 J8
Holmfirth 27 E12
Holsworthy 3 A11
Holt
Norf 24 B5
Wrex 20 A5
Holyhead 18 B2
Holywell 26 H2
Honington 23 A8
Honiton 4 D5
Hook 9 B12
Hook Norton 15 C12
Hope 26 K4
Hopeman 49 A12
Hope under Dinmore 14 A4
Horam 10 H6
Horden 37 J13
Horley 10 E3
Horncastle 29 H11
Horndean 9 F12
Horningsham 8 C3
Hornsea 33 K13
Horrabridge 3 E13
Horringer 25 J3
Horsey 24 C9
Horsford 24 D6
Horsforth 27 B13
Horsham 10 F2
Horsham St Faith 24 D7
Horsted Keynes 10 G4
Horton
Northants 22 K7
Som 4 B7
Horton in Ribblesdale 31 G14
Horwich 26 D7
Houghton-le-Spring 37 H12
Houghton Regis 16 C5
Hounslow 10 B2
Hove 10 J3
Hoveton 24 D7
Hovingham 33 G8
Howden 28 B6
Howpasley 36 C2
Hoxne 24 H6
Hoylake 26 G3
Hucknall 28 K4
Huddersfield 27 D12
Hugh Town 2 C3
Hulland Ward 21 B13
Hullavington 14 H7
Hullbridge 17 F13
Hulme End 27 K12
Humber Bridge 29 B9
Humberston 29 D11
Humshaugh 37 F8
Hundred House 13 A15
Hungerford 15 K12
Hunmanby 33 G12
Hunstanton 24 A1
Huntford 36 C5
Huntingdon 23 H11
Huntley 14 E6
Huntly 50 C4
Hurlford 39 G9
Hurliness 56 H2
Hurn 8 H6
Hursley 9 E9
Hurstbourne Tarrant 9 B8
Hurstpierpoint 10 H3
Hurworth-on-Tees 32 C5
Husbands Bosworth 22 G5
Husinish 55 F2
Huttoft 29 G14
Hutton 26 C5
Hutton Cranswick 33 J12
Hutton-le-Hole 33 E9
Hutton Rudby 32 D6
Huyton 26 F5
Hyde 27 F10
Hynish 42 E1
Hythe
Hants 9 G9
Kent 11 F12

I

Ibsey 8 G6
Ibstock 22 D2
Icklingham 25 H2
Idmiston 8 D7
Ilchester 5 A9
Ilderton 37 A9
Ilfracombe 6 G4
Ilkeston 22 A3
Ilkley 32 K3
Illogan 2 G4
Ilminster 4 B7
Immingham 29 C10
Inchnadamph 52 F4
Inchture 45 F14
Ingatestone 17 F11
Ingleton 31 G12
Ingoldmells 29 H14
Ingram 37 B9
Ingrave 17 F11
Inkberrow 15 A9
Innellan 38 C6
Innerleithen 40 K6
Innermessan 34 G2
Insch 50 E5
Instow 6 J3
Inver 53 K10
Inverallochy 50 A9
Inveran 52 J7
Inveraray 44 J2
Inverarity 51 N3
Inverbervie 51 K7
Invergarry 48 H4
Invergordon 49 B8
Invergowrie 51 P2
Inverie 47 L7
Inverinate 47 J9
Inverkeilor 51 M5
Inverkeithing 40 E4
Inverkirkaig 52 F2
Inverlochlarig 44 H6
Invermoriston 48 G5
Inverness 48 D7
Inversnaid 44 J5
Inverurie 50 E6
Ipswich 25 L6
Irchester 23 J8
Irlam 27 F8
Ironbridge 20 F7
Irthlingborough 23 H8
Irvine 39 G8
Isbister 57 C4
Isleham 25 H1
Isle of Whithorn 34 K5
Islington 10 A4
Islip 15 E14
Ivinghoe 16 D4
Ivybridge 3 F14
Iwerne Minster 8 F3
Ixworth 25 H4

J

Jamestown 39 B8
Jarrow 37 G12
Jaywick 25 P6
Jedburgh 36 A5
John o' Groats 53 A15
Johnshaven 51 L7
Johnston 12 F3
Johnstone 39 D9

K

Kames 38 C4
Kea 2 G5
Kearvaig 52 A4
Kedington 17 A11
Keelby 29 C10
Keele 21 B9
Kegworth 22 C3
Keighley 27 A11
Keillmore 38 B1
Keiss 53 B15
Keith 50 B3
Keld 31 D14
Kellas 49 C12
Kelsale 25 J8
Kelsall 26 J6
Kelso 41 K10
Keltneyburn 45 E9
Kelty 40 D4
Kelvedon 17 D13
Kelynack 2 J1
Kemble 15 G9
Kemnay 50 F6
Kempsey 14 B7
Kempston 16 A5
Kemsing 10 D6
Kendal 31 E11
Kenilworth 22 H1
Kenmore 45 E9
Kennacraig 38 D3
Kennethmont 50 E4
Kennford 4 E3
Kenninghall 24 G5
Kennington 15 F14
Kensington & Chelsea 10 B3
Kentford 25 J2
Kentisbeare 4 C4
Kerry 20 H2
Kerrysdale 46 D8
Kershopefoot 36 E3
Kesgrave 25 L7
Kessingland 24 G10
Keswick 31 B8
Kettering 22 H7
Kettletoft 56 C6
Kettlewell 32 G1
Ketton 23 E8
Kew Bridge 10 B3
Kexby 28 F7
Keyingham 29 B11
Keymer 10 H4
Keynsham 14 K5
Keysoe 23 J9
Keyworth 22 B5
Kibworth Beauchamp 22 F5
Kidderminster 21 J9
Kidlington 15 E14
Kidsgrove 21 A9
Kidstones 32 F1
Kidwelly 12 F8
Kielder 36 D5
Kilberry 38 D2
Kilbirnie 39 E8
Kilcadzow 39 F13
Kilchattan 38 E6
Kilchenzie 38 H1
Kilchiaran 43 M4
Kilchoan 42 B6
Kilchrenan 44 G2
Kilcreggan 38 B7
Kildonan 53 F11
Kilfinan 38 C4
Kilham 33 H12
Kilkhampton 3 A10
Killamarsh 28 F3
Killean 38 F1
Killearn 39 B10
Killin 44 F7
Killinghall 32 J4
Kilmacolm 39 D8
Kilmaluag 46 D4
Kilmany 40 A6
Kilmarnock 39 G9
Kilmartin 38 A3
Kilmaurs 39 F9
Kilmelford 42 G10
Kilmore 42 F10
Kilmory
Argyll 38 C2
Highland 42 A7
Highland 47 L3
Kilmuir 49 A8
Kilninver 42 F10
Kilnsea 29 C13
Kilrenny 41 C8
Kilsby 22 H4
Kilsyth 39 C12
Kilwinning 38 F7
Kimbolton 23 J9
Kimpton 16 D6
Kinbrace 53 F10
Kinbuck 45 J10
Kincardine
Fife 40 E2
Highland 52 K8
Kincardine Bridge 40 E2
Kincraig 49 H9
Kineton 15 A12
Kingarth 38 E5
Kinghorn 40 E5
Kingsbarns 41 B8
Kingsbridge 4 J1
Kingsbury 21 G13
Kingsclere 9 B10
King's Cliffe 23 F9
Kingsdown 11 E14
Kingskerswell 4 G2
Kingsland 20 K5
Kings Langley 16 E5
Kingsley
Hants 9 D12
Staffs 21 B11
King's Lynn 24 D1
King's Somborne 9 D8

King's Sutton 15 C14
Kingsteignton. 4 F2
King's Thorn 14 C4
Kingston
 Devon. 3 G14
 London 10 C2
Kingston Bagpuize . 15 G13
Kingston upon Hull . . 29 B9
Kingswear 4 J2
Kingswood. 14 J5
King's Worthy 9 D10
Kington. 14 A2
Kingussie. 49 H8
Kinloch
 Highland. 47 M4
 Highland. 52 E5
Kinlochbervie 52 C4
Kinlocheil. 47 N9
Kinlochewe 46 E10
Kinlochleven. 44 C3
Kinlochmoidart 42 A9
Kinloch Rannoch 45 D8
Kinloss 49 B11
Kinmel Bay 18 C9
Kinross 40 C4
Kintessack 49 C10
Kintore 50 F6
Kinuachdrachd. 43 J9
Kinver. 21 H9
Kippax. 28 A3
Kippen 39 A11
Kirkabister. 57 J5
Kirkbean. 35 H10
Kirkbride 35 H13
Kirkburton. 27 D12
Kirkby 26 F5
Kirkby-in-Ashfield . . 28 J4
Kirkby-in-Furness. . . 31 F8
Kirkby Lonsdale 31 G12
Kirkby Malzeard 32 G4
Kirkbymoorside 33 F8
Kirkby Stephen. 31 D13
Kirkby Thore 31 B12
Kirkcaldy 40 D5
Kirkcolm. 34 G1
Kirkconnel. 35 B8
Kirkcowan 34 G4
Kirkcudbright 34 H8
Kirkham 26 B5
Kirkinner 34 H5
Kirkintilloch 39 C11
Kirkland 35 D9
Kirkliston. 40 F4
Kirkmichael
 Perth 45 C12
 S Ayrs. 34 C4
Kirk Michael 30 F3
Kirknewton 41 K12
Kirkoswald
 Cumb 36 J4
 S Ayrs. 34 C3
Kirkpatrick Durham . 35 F8
Kirkpatrick Fleming 35 F13
Kirkton of Glenisla . 45 C14
Kirkton of Largo. . . . 40 C7
Kirkwall 56 E4
Kirkwhelpington 37 E9
Kirriemuir 51 M2
Kirtling 25 K1
Kirtlington 15 D14
Kirton 23 B11
Kirton in Lindsey . . . 29 E8
Knaresborough. 32 J5
Knayton 32 F6
Knebworth. 16 D7
Knighton 20 J3
Knott End-on-Sea. . . 31 K9
Knottingley 28 B3
Knowle 21 J12
Knutsford. 27 H8
Kyleakin 47 J7
Kyle of Lochalsh. 47 J7
Kylerhea. 47 J7
Kylestrome 52 E4

L

Laceby 29 D11
Lacock 15 K8
Ladock 2 G6
Ladybank 40 B6
Lagg
 Argyll 43 L7
 N Ayrs 38 H4
Laggan
 Highland. 48 J4
 Highland. 48 J7
 Moray. 50 D2
Laide 46 B9
Lairg 52 H7
Lakenheath 24 G2
Lamberhurst 10 F7
Lambeth 10 B4
Lambley 36 H5
Lambourn 15 J12
Lamlash 38 G5
Lampeter 13 B9
Lanark. 39 F13
Lancaster. 31 H10
Lanchester. 37 J10
Lancing. 10 J2
Landkey 6 J4
Landrake 3 F11
Langford Budville . . . 7 J10
Langham 22 D7
Langholm. 36 E2
Langport. 7 J13
Langsett 27 E13
Langtoft
 E Yorks 33 H12
 Lincs. 23 D10
Langton Matravers . . . 8 K4
Langtree. 6 K3
Langwathby. 31 A11
Langwell. 52 H8
Lanivet 3 E8
Lapford 4 C1
Larbert 39 B13
Largs 38 E7
Larkhall 39 E12
Larkhill 8 C6
Lasswade 40 G6
Latchingdon 17 E13
Latheron. 53 E14
Lauder 41 J8
Laugharne 12 E6
Launceston 3 C11
Laurencekirk. 51 K6
Laurieston 34 G7
Lavendon 23 K8
Lavenham 25 L4
Lawers 45 F8
Laxey. 30 G4
Laxfield. 25 H7
Laxford Bridge 52 D4
Laxton. 28 H6
Layer de la Haye. 25 P4
Lazonby 36 J4
Lea. 28 F7
Leadburn 40 H5
Leadenham 29 J8
Leaden Roding 17 D11
Leadgate 37 H10
Leadhills. 35 B9
Leasingham. 29 K9
Leatherhead 10 D2
Lechlade-on-
 Thames 15 G11
Ledbury 14 C6
Ledmore. 52 G4
Leeds. 27 B13
Leedstown 2 H3
Leek. 27 K10
Leeming Bar 32 E4
Lee-on-the-Solent . . 9 H10
Legbourne 29 F12
Leicester 22 E4
Leigh
 Grt Manchester 26 E7
 Worcs. 14 A6
Leighton Buzzard. . . . 16 C4
Leintwardine. 20 J5
Leiston 25 J9
Leith 40 F5
Leitholm. 41 J10
Lelant 2 H3
Lendalfoot 34 D2
Lenham. 11 D10
Lennoxtown. 39 C11
Leominster 14 A3
Lephin. 46 G1
Le Planel . . . . 4 Guern
Lerwick. 57 H5
Lesbury. 37 B11
Leslie. 40 C5
Lesmahagow. 39 F13
Leswalt. 34 G1
Letchworth 16 B7
Lettan 56 B7
Letterston 12 D3
Lettoch. 49 E12
Leuchars 40 A7
Leumrabhagh 55 F5
Leven
 E Yorks 33 K13
 Fife. 40 C6
Leverburgh / An t-
 Ob 55 J2
Lewes 10 J5
Lewisham. 10 B4
Lewiston. 48 F6
Leyburn 32 E3
Leyland 26 C6
Leysdown-on-Sea . . 11 C11
Lhanbryde 49 B13
Liatrie 48 E3
Lichfield 21 F12
Lidgate 25 K2
Lifton. 3 C11
Lilleshall. 21 E8
Lincoln 29 G8
Lindale 31 F10
Lingfield. 10 E4
Linkinhorne. 3 D11
Linksness 56 F2
Linlithgow 40 F2
Linslade 16 C4
Linton 17 A10
Liphook 9 E13
Liskeard 3 E10
Liss 9 E12
Lissett. 33 J13
Litcham 24 D3
Litherland 26 F4
Littleborough 27 D10
Littlehampton. 10 J1
Littlemill. 49 C10
Littleport 23 G14
Little Shelford. 23 K13
Littlestone-on-Sea 11 G11
Little Stukeley. 23 H11
Little Walsingham . . . 24 B4
Liverpool 26 G4
Liverpool Airport 26 G5
Livingston 40 G3
Lizard 2 K4
Llanaber. 19 J5
Llanaelhaiarn 18 F3
Llanafan-fawr. 19 Q9
Llanarmon 26 K2
Llanarmon Dyffryn
 Ceiriog 20 C2
Llanarth 19 Q4
Llanarthne. 13 E9
Llanbadarn Fynydd . . 20 J2
Llanbedr. 18 H5
Llanbedrog 18 G3
Llanberis 18 E5
Llanbister. 20 J2
Llanbrynmair 19 K9
Llanddewi-Brefi 19 Q6
Llanddulas. 18 C8
Llandeilo 13 D10
Llandinam 19 M10
Llandissilio 12 D5
Llandogo 14 F4
Llandovery. 13 C11
Llandrillo 18 G10
Llandrindod Wells . . 19 P10
Llandudno 18 B7
Llandybie 13 E10
Llandyfriog 12 B7
Llandygwydd. 12 B6
Llandyrnog 26 J2
Llandysul 12 B8
Llanelidan 20 B1
Llanelli 13 F9
Llanelltyd. 19 J7
Llanenddwyn. 18 H5
Llanerchymedd. 18 B4
Llanerfyl. 19 K10
Llanfaethlu 18 B3
Llanfair Caereinion . . 20 F2
Llanfairfechan 18 C6
Llanfairpwllgwngyll . 18 C5
Llanfair Talhaiarn. . . . 18 C9
Llanfechain 20 E2
Llanfechell. 18 B3
Llan Ffestiniog 18 F7
Llanfihangel-ar-arth 13 C8
Llanfrynach 13 D14
Llanfyllin 20 E2
Llangadfan. 19 J10
Llangadog 13 D11
Llangammarch
 Wells. 13 B13
Llangefni 18 C4
Llangeitho 19 Q6
Llangelynin 19 K5
Llangennech 13 F9
Llangernyw 18 D8
Llanglydwen 12 D5
Llangoed 18 C6
Llangollen 20 B3
Llangorse. 13 D15
Llangranog 12 A7
Llangunllo 20 J3
Llangurig 19 N9
Llangwm 14 F3
Llangybi 19 Q6
Llangynidr 13 E15
Llangynog 18 H10
Llanharan. 7 C9
Llanidloes 19 M9
Llanilar 19 N6
Llanllyfni 18 E4
Llannor. 18 G3
Llanon. 19 P5
Llanpumsaint 12 D8
Llanrhaeadr-ym-
 Mochnant 20 D2
Llanrhian 12 C2
Llanrhidian 13 G8
Llanrhystyd 19 N5
Llanrug. 18 D5
Llanrwst 18 D7
Llansannan 18 D9
Llansawel. 13 C10
Llanstephan. 12 E7
Llanthony. 14 D1
Llantrisant 7 C9
Llantwit-Major 13 K13
Llanuwchllyn. 18 G8
Llanvihangel
 Crucorney 14 D2
Llanwddyn 19 J10
Llanwenog. 13 B8
Llanwrda 13 C11
Llanwrtyd Wells 13 B12
Llanybledwel. 20 D3
Llanybydder. 13 B9
Llanymynech. 20 D3
Llanystumdwy. 18 G4
Llay 20 A4
Lledrod 19 N6
Llithfaen. 18 F3
Llwyngwril. 19 J6
Llyswen 13 C15
Loanhead 40 G5
Lochailort 47 N7
Lochaline 42 D8
Lochans 34 H1
Locharbriggs. 35 E10
Loch Baghasdail /
 Lochboisdale 54 H4
Lochboisdale / Loch
 Baghasdail 54 H4
Lochbuie 42 F8
Lochcarron 46 G9
Loch Choire Lodge . . 52 E8
Lochdon 42 E9
Lochearnhead. 44 G7
Loch Euphoirt. 54 C5
Lochgair. 38 A4
Lochgelly 40 D4
Lochgilphead 38 B3
Lochgoilhead 44 J4
Lochinver. 52 F2
Lochmaben 35 E11
Lochmaddy / Loch nam
 Madadh 54 C6
Loch nam Madadh /
 Lochmaddy 54 C6
Lochranza 38 E4
Loch Sgioport. 54 F5
Lochwinnoch 39 D8
Lockerbie. 35 E12
Lockton 33 E10
Loddiswell 4 J1
Loddon 24 F8
Loftus 33 C9
Logan 34 A7
London 10 B4
London Colney 16 E6
Long Ashton 14 K4
Long Bennington. . . . 22 A7
Longbenton. 37 G11
Longbridge Deverill . . 8 C3
Long Clawson 22 C6
Long Compton 15 C11
Long Crendon 16 E1
Longdon. 14 C7
Long Eaton 22 B3
Longford 14 D7
Longforgan 51 P2
Longformacus. 41 H10
Longframlington . . . 37 C10
Longhope. 56 G3
Longhorsley 37 D10
Longhoughton 37 B11
Long Itchington 22 J3
Long Melford 25 L3
Longnor 27 J11
Long Preston. 31 J14
Longridge 26 B7
Longside 50 C9
Long Stratton 24 F6
Long Sutton. 23 C13
Longtown
 Cumb 36 G2
 Hereford 14 D2
Loose 11 D8
Lossiemouth 49 A13
Lostock Gralam 26 H8
Lostwithiel. 3 F8
Loth. 56 C6
Loughborough 22 C4
Loughor 13 G9
Loughton 17 F9
Louth. 29 F12
Lowdham 22 A5
Lower Beeding 10 G3
Lower Killeyan 43 P4
Lower Langford 7 F13
Lower Mayland. 17 E14
Lower Shiplake. 16 H2
Lowestoft. 24 F10
Lowick 41 J13
Loxwood. 10 F1
Lubcroy. 52 H5
Lucker. 41 K14
Ludborough. 29 E11
Ludford. 29 F10
Ludgershall 8 B7
Ludgvan 2 H2
Ludham 24 D8
Ludlow 20 J6
Lugton 39 E9
Lugwardine 14 B4
Lumphanan 50 G4
Lumsden 50 E3
Luss 39 A8
Lusta 46 F2
Luton. 16 C5
Lutterworth 22 G4
Lutton. 23 G10
Lybster 53 E14

Lydd....................11 H11
Lydd on Sea.......11 H11
Lydford...............3 C13
Lydham...............20 G4
Lydney................14 F5
Lyme Regis...........4 D7
Lyminge..............11 E12
Lymington............9 H8
Lymm.................26 G7
Lympne................11 F12
Lympstone............4 E3
Lyndhurst.............8 G7
Lyneham..............15 J9
Lyness.................56 G3
Lynmouth..............6 G6
Lynton.................6 G6
Lytchett Minster.....8 H4
Lytham St Anne's....26 C4
Lythe..................33 C10

M

Mablethorpe........29 F13
Macclesfield........27 H10
Macduff..............50 A5
Machen.................7 C11
Machrihanish........38 H1
Machynlleth.........19 K7
Macmerry.............40 F7
Madeley..............21 B8
Madley...............14 C3
Maentwrog...........18 G6
Maesteg..............13 H12
Maghull..............26 E4
Magor................14 H3
Maiden Bradley......8 D3
Maidenhead..........16 H3
Maiden Newton.......5 D9
Maidstone...........11 D8
Maldon...............17 E13
Malham...............31 H14
Mallaig...............47 M6
Mallwyd..............19 J8
Malmesbury..........15 H8
Malpas................20 B6
Maltby...............28 E4
Maltby le Marsh....29 F13
Malton...............33 G9
Manafon..............20 F2
Manby................29 F13
Manchester...........27 F9
Manchester Airport..27 G9
Manea................23 G13
Mangotsfield........14 J5
Manningtree.........25 M6
Manorbier...........12 G4
Mansfield............28 H4
Mansfield
  Woodhouse.........28 H4
Manton...............22 E7
Marazion..............2 J3
Marbhig..............55 F6
March................23 F13
Marden
  Hereford...........14 B4
  Kent................11 E8
Mareham le Fen.....29 H11
Maresfield...........10 G5
Marfleet.............29 B10
Margam...............13 H11
Margate..............11 C14
Marham...............24 D2
Market Bosworth....22 E3
Market Deeping......23 D10
Market Drayton......20 C7
Market Harborough..22 G6
Market Lavington.....8 B5
Market Rasen.......29 F10
Market Warsop.......28 H4
Market Weighton....33 K10
Markfield............22 D3
Markinch.............40 C6
Marks Tey...........25 N4
Markyate.............16 D5

Marlborough
  Devon................4 K1
  Wilts...............15 K10
Marlow................16 G3
Marnhull..............5 B11
Marple...............27 G10
Marshchapel........29 E12
Marshfield...........14 J6
Marske-by-the-Sea..33 B8
Marston Magna........5 A9
Martham..............24 D9
Martin.................8 F5
Martley..............21 K8
Martock................5 B8
Marton................28 F7
Marykirk.............51 L5
Marypark.............49 E12
Maryport.............35 K11
Mary Tavy.............3 D13
Marywell
  Aberds..............51 H4
  Angus...............51 N5
Masham...............32 F4
Mathry................12 C2
Matlock...............28 H1
Mattishall...........24 D5
Mauchline............39 H9
Maud.................50 C8
Maughold.............30 F4
Mawgan................2 J5
Mawnan.................2 J5
Maxwellheugh.......41 K10
Maybole..............34 C4
Mayfield
  E Sus...............10 G6
  Staffs..............21 B12
Mealabost...........55 D6
Mealsgate...........35 J13
Measham..............22 D2
Medstead..............9 D11
Meidrim..............12 E6
Meifod................20 E2
Meigle................51 N1
Melbourn.............17 A8
Melbourne............22 C2
Melgarve.............48 J5
Melksham..............8 A4
Mellon Charles......46 B8
Mellor................26 B7
Melmerby.............36 K5
Melrose..............41 K8
Melsonby.............32 D3
Meltham..............27 D12
Melton................25 K7
Melton Constable....24 B5
Melton Mowbray.....22 D6
Melvaig..............46 C7
Melvich..............53 B10
Menai Bridge........18 C5
Mendlesham..........25 J6
Mennock..............35 C9
Menston..............27 A12
Menstrie............39 A13
Meonstoke............9 F11
Meopham..............17 J11
Mere..................8 D3
Mere Brow...........26 D5
Meriden..............21 H13
Merriott..............5 B8
Merthyr Tydfil......13 F14
Merton................10 C3
Meshaw................6 K6
Messingham..........28 D7
Metfield.............24 G7
Metheringham........29 H9
Methil...............40 C6
Methlick.............50 D7
Methven..............45 G12
Methwold.............24 F2
Mevagissey............3 G8
Mexborough..........28 D3
Mey..................53 A14
Micheldever..........9 D10
Michelmersh..........9 E8
Mickleover...........22 B2
Mickleton
  Durham.............32 B1
  Glos................15 B10
Midbea...............56 B4

Middle Barton......15 D13
Middleham...........32 F3
Middlemarsh..........5 C10
Middlesbrough......32 B7
Middleton
  Argyll..............42 D1
  Grt Manchester.....27 E9
  Norf................24 D1
Middleton Cheney...15 B14
Middleton-in-
  Teesdale...........32 B1
Middleton-on-Sea....9 H14
Middleton on the
  Wolds.............33 K11
Middlewich..........26 J8
Middlezoy............7 H12
Midhurst.............9 E13
Mid Lavant...........9 G13
Midsomer Norton.....8 B1
Mid Yell.............57 C6
Milborne Port........5 B10
Mildenhall..........24 H2
Milford..............9 C14
Milford Haven.......12 F2
Milford on Sea.......8 H7
Millbrook............3 F12
Millom...............30 F7
Millport.............38 E6
Milnathort..........40 C4
Milngavie...........39 C10
Milnthorpe..........31 F11
Milovaig............46 F1
Milton...............48 C4
Milton Abbot.........3 D11
Milton Keynes.......16 B3
Milverton.............7 J10
Minchinhampton.....14 G7
Minehead.............7 G8
Minera...............20 A3
Minety...............15 H9
Minnigaff...........34 G5
Minster
  Kent...............11 B10
  Kent...............11 C14
Minsterley...........20 F4
Mintlaw..............50 C9
Mirfield.............27 D13
Misterton
  Notts..............28 E6
  Som.................5 C8
Mistley..............25 M6
Mitcheldean.........14 E5
Mitchel Troy........14 F3
Modbury..............3 F14
Moelfre..............18 B5
Moffat..............35 C11
Mold..................26 J3
Monar Lodge.........48 D3
Moniaive............35 D8
Monifieth...........51 P4
Monikie.............51 N4
Monkland............14 A3
Monkokehampton......3 A13
Monkton.............39 H8
Monmouth............14 E4
Montacute............5 B8
Montgomery...........20 G3
Montrose.............51 M6
Monymusk.............50 F5
Morar................47 M6
Morchard Bishop......4 C1
Mordiford...........14 C4
Morebattle..........36 A6
Morecambe...........31 H10
Moretonhampstead.....4 E1
Moreton-in-Marsh...15 C11
Morley...............27 C13
Morpeth..............37 E11
Mortehoe.............6 G3
Mortimer's Cross....20 K5
Morwenstow...........6 K1
Mossley..............27 E10
Mostyn...............26 H2
Motcombe.............8 E3
Motherwell..........39 D12
Mottisfont...........9 E8
Moulton
  Lincs..............23 C12
  Northants..........22 J7

Moulton continued
  Suff................25 J2
Mountain Ash.........7 B9
Mountsorrel.........22 D4
Mousehole.............2 J2
Mouswald............35 F11
Moy..................49 E8
Muchalls.............51 H7
Much Dewchurch......14 D3
Much Marcle.........14 C5
Much Wenlock........20 F7
Muir.................49 K11
Muirdrum............51 P4
Muirhead............39 D12
Muirkirk.............39 H12
Muir of Ord.........48 C6
Muker................32 E1
Mulben...............50 B2
Mullion...............2 K4
Mullion Cove.........2 K4
Mundesley...........24 B7
Mundford............24 F3
Munlochy............48 C7
Murlaggan..........47 M10
Murton...............37 J13
Musbury..............4 D6
Musselburgh.........40 F6
Muthill..............45 H10
Mybster..............53 C13
Myddle...............20 D5
Mydroilyn............19 Q4
Mynydd Isa...........26 J3

N

Nafferton...........33 J12
Nailsea...............7 D13
Nailsworth..........14 G7
Nairn................49 C9
Nannerch............26 H2
Nantwich.............20 A7
Nappa................31 J14
Narberth.............12 E5
Narborough..........22 F4
Naseby...............22 H5
Navenby.............29 J8
Neap.................57 G6
Neath................13 G11
Necton...............24 E3
Needham Market......25 K5
Needingworth........23 H17
Nefyn................18 G3
Neilston.............39 E9
Nelson...............27 B9
Nenthead.............36 J6
Neston...............26 H3
Netheravon...........8 C6
Netherbury...........5 D8
Nether Stowey........7 H10
Netherthird..........34 B6
Netherton............37 C8
Nethy Bridge........49 F11
Netley................9 G9
Nettlebed...........16 G2
Nettleham............29 G9
Nettleton............29 E10
Nevern...............12 C4
New Abbey...........35 G10
New Aberdour........50 A7
New Alresford........9 D11
Newark-on-Trent.....28 J7
New Ash Green.......10 C7
Newbiggin-by-the-
  Sea................37 E12
Newbigging..........40 J3
Newborough..........18 D4
Newbridge............7 B11
Newbridge on Wye...19 Q10
Newbrough...........36 G7
New Buckenham.......24 F5
Newburgh
  Aberds.............50 E8
  Fife................40 B5
Newburn.............37 G10
Newbury.............15 K13
Newby Bridge........31 F9
Newbyth..............50 B7
Newcastle............20 H3

Newcastle Emlyn....12 C7
Newcastleton........36 E3
Newcastle-under-
  Lyme...............21 B9
Newcastle-upon-
  Tyne...............37 G11
Newchurch...........14 A1
New Costessey.......24 D6
New Cumnock.........34 B7
New Deer.............50 C7
Newdigate...........10 E2
New Earswick........33 J8
New Edlington......28 E4
Newent...............14 D6
Newgale.............12 D2
New Galloway........34 F7
Newham...............10 A5
Newhaven............10 J5
New Holland.........29 B9
Newick...............10 G5
Newington
  Kent...............11 C9
  Kent...............11 F12
Newlot...............56 E5
New Luce............34 G2
Newlyn................2 J2
Newmachar..........50 E7
Newmarket
  Suff................25 J1
  W Isles............55 D6
Newmill..............50 B3
New Mills...........27 G11
Newmilns............39 G10
New Milton............8 H7
Newnham.............14 E5
New Pitsligo........50 B7
Newport
  Essex..............17 B10
  IoW.................9 J10
  Newport.............7 C12
  Pembs..............12 C4
  Telford............21 D8
Newport-on-Tay.....40 A7
Newport Pagnell....16 A3
Newquay..............2 E5
New Quay............19 Q3
New Radnor..........20 K3
New Romney..........11 G11
New Rossington.....28 E5
New Scone..........45 G13
Newton..............31 J13
Newton Abbot.........4 F2
Newton Arlosh......35 H12
Newton Aycliffe....32 B4
Newton Ferrers......3 G13
Newtongrange.......40 G6
Newtonhill..........51 H8
Newton le Willows..26 F6
Newton Mearns......39 E10
Newtonmore.........49 J8
Newton Poppleford...4 E4
Newton St Cyres......4 D2
Newton Stewart.....34 G5
Newtown
  Hants...............8 G7
  Hereford...........14 B5
  Powys..............20 G2
Newtown St
  Boswells...........41 K8
New Tredegar.........7 A10
New Waltham........29 D11
Neyland..............12 F3
Ninfield.............11 H8
Niton.................9 K10
Nordelph.............23 E14
Norham...............41 J9
Normanby le Wold...29 E10
Normanton...........28 B3
Northallerton.......32 E5
Northam...............6 J3
Northampton.........22 J6
North Baddesley......9 F8
North Berwick.......41 E8
North Cerney........15 F9
Northchapel..........9 E14
North Charlton.....37 A10
North Elmham........24 C4
North Ferriby.......29 B8
Northfleet..........17 H11

North Frodingham 33 J12
North Hill 3 D10
North Hykeham 29 H8
Northiam 11 G9
North Kessock 48 D7
Northleach 15 E10
North Molton 6 J6
North Newbald 29 A8
Northop 26 J3
North Petherton 7 H11
Northpunds 57 K5
North Queensferry 40 E4
Northrepps 24 B7
North Somercotes 29 E13
North Tawton 3 B14
North Thoresby 29 E11
North Walsham 24 B7
Northwich 26 H7
North Wingfield 28 H3
Northwold 24 F2
Northwood
IoW 9 H9
London 16 F5
Norton
Glos 14 D7
N Yorks 33 G9
Suff 25 J4
Worcs 14 A7
Norton Fitzwarren 7 J10
Norwich 24 E7
Norwick 57 A7
Nottingham 22 B4
Nuneaton 22 F2
Nunney 8 C2
Nutley 10 G5
Nybster 53 B15

O

Oadby 22 E5
Oakdale 7 B10
Oakengates 21 E8
Oakham 22 E7
Oakley 40 E3
Oban 42 E10
Ochiltree 34 A6
Ockley 10 F2
Odie 56 D6
Odiham 9 C12
Offord D'Arcy 23 J11
Ogbourne St George 15 J10
Okehampton 3 B13
Old Basing 9 B11
Old Bolingbroke 29 H12
Oldbury 14 G5
Old Colwyn 18 C8
Old Deer 50 C8
Old Fletton 23 F10
Oldham 27 E10
Old Leake 29 K12
Oldmeldrum 50 E7
Old Radnor 14 A1
Olgrinmore 53 C12
Ollaberry 57 D4
Ollerton 28 H5
Olney 22 K7
Ombersley 21 K9
Onchan 30 H3
Onich 44 C2
Opinan 46 B8
Ordhead 50 F5
Ordie 50 G3
Orford 25 K9
Orleton 20 K6
Ormesby St Margaret 24 D9
Ormiston 40 G7
Ormskirk 26 D5
Orpington 10 C5
Orton 31 D12
Osbournby 23 B9
Oskamull 42 D6
Osmotherley 32 E6
Ossett 27 D13
Oswaldtwistle 27 C8
Oswestry 20 D3
Otford 10 D6
Othery 7 H12
Otley 32 K3
Otterburn 36 D7
Otter Ferry 38 B4
Otterton 4 E4
Ottery St Mary 4 D4
Oulton 24 F10
Oulton Broad 24 F10
Oundle 23 G9
Ousdale 53 G12
Outwell 23 E14
Over 23 H12
Overbister 56 B6
Overseal 21 E13
Overstrand 24 B7
Overton
Hants 9 C10
Wrex 20 B4
Over Wallop 8 D7
Owston Ferry 28 E7
Oxenholme 31 F11
Oxford 15 F14
Oxnam 36 B6
Oxted 10 D4
Oykel Bridge 52 H5

P

Pabail 55 D7
Paddock Wood 10 E7
Padiham 27 B9
Padstow 2 D7
Paibeil 54 C4
Paignton 4 H2
Pailton 22 G3
Painscastle 13 B15
Painshawfield 37 H9
Painswick 14 F7
Paisley 39 D9
Palgrave 24 H6
Palnackie 35 H9
Pangbourne 16 H1
Papworth Everard 23 J11
Parkeston 25 M7
Parkhurst 9 H9
Parracombe 6 G5
Partney 29 H13
Parton 30 B5
Pateley Bridge 32 H3
Pathhead 40 G7
Patna 34 B5
Patrick Brompton 32 E4
Patrington 29 B12
Patterdale 31 C9
Paull 29 B10
Paulton 8 B1
Peacehaven 10 J5
Peak Forest 27 H12
Peasedown St John 8 B2
Peasenhall 25 J8
Peasmarsh 11 G10
Peebles 40 J5
Peel 30 G2
Pegswood 37 E11
Peinchorran 47 H5
Pembrey 12 F8
Pembridge 14 A3
Pembroke 12 F3
Pembroke Dock 12 F3
Pembury 10 F7
Penally 12 G5
Penarth 7 D10
Pencader 12 C8
Pencoed 13 H13
Pendeen 2 H1
Penderyn 13 F13
Pendine 12 F6
Penicuik 40 G5
Penistone 27 E13
Penkridge 21 E10
Penmachno 18 F7
Penmaenmawr 18 C7
Pennan 50 A7
Pennyghael 42 F7
Penpont 35 D9
Penrhyndeudraeth 18 G6
Penrith 31 A11
Penryn 2 H5
Pensford 8 A1
Penshaw 37 H12
Penshurst 10 E6
Pensilva 3 E10
Pentraeth 18 C5
Pentrefoelas 18 E8
Penybont 20 K2
Penybontfawr 20 D1
Pen-y-gop 18 F9
Penygroes
Carms 13 E9
Gwyn 18 E4
Penysarn 18 B4
Penzance 2 J2
Perranporth 2 F5
Perranzabuloe 2 G5
Pershore 15 B8
Perth 45 G13
Peterborough 23 F10
Peterchurch 14 C2
Peterculter 50 G7
Peterhead 50 C10
Peterlee 37 J13
Petersfield 9 E12
Petworth 9 E14
Pevensey 10 J7
Pewsey 8 B6
Pickering 33 F9
Piddletrenthide 5 D11
Pidley 23 H12
Pierowall 56 B4
Pilling 31 K10
Pilton 7 H14
Pinchbeck 23 C11
Pinhoe 4 D3
Pinmore Mains 34 D3
Pinwherry 34 E3
Pirbright 9 B14
Pirnmill 38 F3
Pitlochry 45 D11
Pittenweem 41 C8
Plean 39 B13
Plockton 47 H8
Pluckley 11 E10
Plumpton 36 K4
Plymouth 3 F12
Plympton 3 F13
Plymstock 3 F13
Pocklington 33 K10
Polegate 10 J6
Polesworth 21 F13
Polloch 42 B10
Polperro 3 G9
Polruan 3 G9
Polwarth 41 H10
Polzeath 2 D7
Pontardawe 13 F11
Pontardulais 13 F9
Pontefract 28 B3
Ponteland 37 F10
Ponterwyd 19 M7
Pontesbury 20 F5
Pontrhydfendigaid 19 P7
Pontrilas 14 D3
Pontyates 13 F8
Pontyberem 13 E8
Pontypool 7 A11
Pontypridd 7 C9
Pool 2 G4
Poole 8 J5
Poolewe 46 D8
Pooley Bridge 31 B10
Porlock 6 G7
Port Appin 44 E1
Port Askaig 43 M6
Portavadie 38 C4
Port Bannatyne 38 D5
Port Carlisle 35 G13
Port Charlotte 43 N4
Port Ellen 43 P5
Portencross 38 F6
Port Erin 30 J2
Port Eynon 13 H8
Port Glasgow 39 C8
Portgordon 50 A2
Porth 7 B9
Porthcawl 13 J12
Port Henderson 46 D7
Porthleven 2 J4
Porthmadog 18 G5
Port Isaac 2 D7
Portishead 14 J3
Portknockie 50 A3
Portlethen 51 H8
Port Logan 34 J2
Portmahomack 53 K11
Portnacroish 44 E1
Portnahaven 43 N3
Portnalong 47 H3
Port Nan Giuran 55 D7
Port Nan Long 54 B6
Port Nis 55 A7
Porton 8 D6
Portpatrick 34 H1
Port Ramsay 42 D10
Portreath 2 G4
Portree 46 G4
Port St Mary 30 J2
Portskerra 53 B10
Portslade-by-Sea 10 J3
Portsmouth 9 H11
Portsoy 50 A4
Port Talbot 13 H11
Port William 34 J4
Postbridge 3 D14
Potter Heigham 24 D9
Potterne 8 B4
Potters Bar 16 E7
Potterspury 16 A2
Potton 16 A7
Poulton-le-Fylde 26 B4
Poundstock 3 B9
Powick 14 A7
Poynton 27 G10
Praa Sands 2 J3
Prees 20 C6
Preesall 31 K9
Presbury 27 H10
Prescot 26 F5
Prestatyn 26 G1
Prestbury 15 D8
Presteigne 20 K4
Preston
Borders 41 H10
Dorset 5 E10
E Yorks 29 A10
Kent 11 C13
Lancs 26 B6
Preston Candover 9 C11
Prestonpans 40 F6
Prestwich 27 E9
Prestwick 34 A4
Prestwood 16 E3
Princes Risborough 16 E3
Princetown 3 D13
Probus 2 G6
Prudhoe 37 G9
Pubil 44 E6
Pucklechurch 14 J5
Puddletown 5 D11
Pudsey 27 B13
Pulborough 10 H1
Pulham Market 24 G6
Pulham St Mary 24 G7
Pumpsaint 13 B10
Purfleet 17 H10
Purley
London 10 C4
W Berks 16 H1
Purton 15 H9
Puttenham 9 C14
Pwllheli 18 G3
Pyle 13 H12

Q

Quadring 23 B11
Quainton 16 D2
Quedgeley 14 E7
Queenborough 11 B10
Queensbury 27 C12
Queensferry
Edin 40 F4
Flint 26 J4
Quorndon 22 D4

R

Rackenford 4 B2
Rackheath 24 D7
Rackwick 56 G2
Radcliffe 27 E8
Radcliffe-on-Trent 22 B5
Radlett 16 F6
Radley 15 G14
Radstock 8 B1
Radyr 7 C10
Raglan 14 F3
Rainham 11 C9
Rainworth 28 J5
Rampside 31 H8
Ramsbottom 27 D8
Ramsey
Cambs 23 G11
Essex 25 M7
IoM 30 F4
Ramseycleuch 35 B13
Ramsgate 11 C14
Rannoch Station 44 D6
Rapness 56 B5
Rathen 50 A9
Rattray 45 E13
Raunds 23 H8
Ravenglass 30 E6
Ravenshead 28 J4
Ravenstonedale 31 D13
Rawcliffe 32 J7
Rawmarsh 28 E3
Rawtenstall 27 C9
Rayleigh 17 F13
Reading 16 H2
Reay 53 B11
Redbourn 16 D6
Redbridge 17 G9
Redcar 33 B8
Red Dial 35 J13
Redditch 21 K11
Redesmouth 36 E7
Redhill 10 E3
Red Houses 5 Jersey
Redland 56 D3
Redlynch 8 F7
Redmile 22 B7
Redmire 32 E2
Red Point 46 E7
Redruth 2 G4
Reedham 24 E9
Reepham 24 C5
Reeth 32 E2
Reigate 10 E3
Reiss 53 C15
Renfrew 39 D10
Rennington 37 B11
Repton 22 C2
Resolven 13 F12
Reston 41 G11
Retford 28 F6
Reydon 24 H10
Rhayader 19 P9
Rhewl 26 J2
Rhiconich 52 C4
Rhiw 18 H2
Rhondda 13 G13
Rhoose 7 E9
Rhoslan 18 F4
Rhosllanerchrugog 20 B3
Rhosneigr 18 C3
Rhos-on-Sea 18 B8
Rhossili 12 H8
Rhostryfan 18 E4
Rhubodach 38 C5
Rhuddlan 18 C10
Rhyd-Ddu 18 E5
Rhyl 18 B10
Rhymney 13 F15
Rhynie 50 E3
Riccall 28 A5
Richmond
London 10 B2
N Yorks 32 D3

Rickmansworth 16 F5
Ridsdale 37 E8
Rievaulx 32 F7
Rigside 39 G13
Rillington 33 G10
Ringford 34 H7
Ringmer 10 H5
Ringwood 8 G6
Ripley
Derbys 28 J3
N Yorks 32 H4
Sur 10 D1
Ripon 32 G5
Ripponden 27 C11
Risca 7 C11
Rishton 27 B8
Roade 22 K6
Roadhead 36 F4
Roberton 36 B3
Robertsbridge 11 G8
Robin Hood's Bay 33 D11
Rocester 21 C12
Rochdale 27 D9
Roche 2 F7
Rochester
Medway 17 J12
Northumb 36 D7
Rochford 17 G13
Rockcliffe
Cumb 36 G2
Dumfries 35 H9
Rockingham 22 F7
Rogart 53 H9
Rogate 9 E13
Roghadal 55 J2
Rolvenden 11 F9
Romford 17 G10
Romsey 9 E8
Ropsley 23 B9
Rosedale Abbey 33 E9
Rosehall 52 H6
Rosehearty 50 A8
Rosemarket 12 F3
Rosemarkie 49 C8
Roskhill 46 G2
Roslin 40 G5
Rosneath 38 B7
Ross 41 K14
Rossett 26 K4
Ross-On-Wye 14 D5
Rosyth 40 E4
Rothbury 37 C9
Rotherham 28 E3
Rothes 49 D13
Rothesay 38 D5
Rothienorman 50 D6
Rothiesholm 56 D6
Rothwell
Northants 22 G7
W Yorks 28 B2
Rottal 51 K2
Rottingdean 10 J4
Rowanburn 36 F3
Rowlands Gill 37 H10
Roxburgh 41 K10
Roxby 29 C8
Royal Leamington Spa 22 J2
Royal Tunbridge Wells 10 F6
Royal Wootton Bassett 15 H9
Roybridge 44 A4
Royston
Herts 17 A8
S Yorks 28 D2
Royton 27 E10
Ruabon 20 B4
Ruan Minor 2 K5
Ruardean 14 E5
Rubery 21 J10
Rudston 33 H12
Rufford 26 D5
Rugby 22 H4
Rugeley 21 E11
Ruislip 16 G6
Rumburgh 24 G8
Rumney 7 D11
Runcorn 26 G6
Rushden 23 J8
Rushwick 14 A7
Ruskington 29 J9
Rutherglen 39 D11
Ruthin 26 K2
Ruthven 49 H8
Ruthwell 35 G11
Ryal 37 F9
Rydal 31 D9
Ryde 9 H10
Rye 11 G10
Ryhall 23 D9
Ryhope 37 H13
Ryton 22 H2

S

Sacriston 37 J11
Saddell 38 G2
Saffron Walden 17 B10
Sageston 12 F4
St Abb's 41 G12
St Agnes 2 G5
St Albans 16 E6
St Andrews 41 B8
St Ann's 35 D11
St Arvans 14 G4
St Asaph 18 C10
St Athan 7 E9
St Aubin 5 Jersey
St Austell 3 F8
St Bees 30 C5
St Blazey 3 F8
St Breward 3 D8
St Briavels 14 F4
St Bride's Major 13 J12
St Buryan 2 J1
St Clears 12 E6
St Columb Major 2 E6
St Columb Minor 2 E6
St Combs 50 A9
St Cyrus 51 L6
St David's 12 D1
St Day 2 G5
St Dennis 2 F7
St Dogmaels 12 B5
St Dominick 3 E11
St Enoder 2 F6
St Erth 2 H3
St Fergus 50 B9
St Fillans 45 G8
St Germans 3 F11
St Harmon 19 N9
St Helens 26 F6
St Helier 5 Jersey
St Issey 2 D7
St Ives
Cambs 23 H12
Corn 2 H3
St John's
IoM 30 G2
Jersey 5 Jersey
St Johns Chapel 31 A14
St John's Town of Dalry 34 E7
St Just 2 H1
St Keverne 2 K5
St Leonards 11 J9
St Levan 2 J1
St Mabyn 3 D8
St Margaret's-at-Cliffe 11 E14
St Margaret's Hope 56 G4
St Martin's 5 Jersey
St Mary Bourne 9 B9
St Mary's 56 F4
St Mary's Bay 11 G11
St Mawes 2 H6
St Mellons 7 D11
St Merryn 2 D6
St Minver 2 D7
St Monance 41 C8
St Neots 23 J10
St Newlyn East 2 F6
St Olaves 24 F9
St Osyth 25 P6
St Ouens 5 Jersey
St Peter Port 4 Guern
St Peter's 5 Jersey
St Sampson 4 Guern
St Stephen 2 F7
St Teath 3 D8
St Tudy 3 D8
Salcombe 4 K1
Sale 27 F8
Salen
Argyll 42 D7
Highland 42 B8
Salford 27 F9
Salford Priors 15 A9
Saline 40 D3
Salisbury 8 E6
Sallachy 52 H7
Saltash 3 F12
Saltburn-by-the-Sea 33 B8
Saltcoats 38 F7
Saltfleet 29 E13
Saltfleetby 29 E13
Saltwood 11 F12
Sampford Courtenay 3 B14
Sanaigmore 43 L4
Sandbach 27 J8
Sandbank 38 C6
Sandgate 11 F13
Sandhead 34 J2
Sandhurst 16 J3
Sandleigh 15 F13
Sandness 57 G2
Sandown 9 J10
Sandringham 24 B1
Sandwich 11 D14
Sandy 16 A6
Sanquhar 35 B8
Sarnau 12 A7
Sarnesfield 14 A2
Sarre 11 C13
Satterthwaite 31 E9
Saundersfoot 12 F5
Sawbridgeworth 17 D9
Sawston 17 A9
Sawtry 23 G10
Saxilby 29 G8
Saxlingham Nethergate 24 F7
Saxmundham 25 J8
Saxthorpe 24 B6
Scalasaig 43 J5
Scalby 33 F12
Scalloway 57 J4
Scalpay 55 H4
Scamblesby 29 G11
Scarborough 33 F12
Scardoy 48 C3
Scarinish 42 D2
Scarning 24 D4
Scole 24 H6
Sconser 47 H5
Scopwick 29 J9
Scorton 32 D4
Scotch Corner 32 D4
Scotter 28 D7
Scourie 52 D3
Scousburgh 57 L4
Scrabster 53 B13
Scremerston 41 J13
Scunthorpe 28 C7
Seaford 10 K5
Seaham 37 J13
Seahouses 41 K15
Seamer 33 F12
Sea Palling 24 C9
Seascale 30 D6
Seaton
Cumb 30 A6
Devon 4 E6
Seaton Delaval 37 F12
Seaview 9 H11
Sebergham 36 J2
Sedbergh 31 E12
Sedgefield 32 A5
Seend 8 B4
Selborne 9 D12
Selby 28 A5
Selkirk 36 A3
Sellafield 30 D6
Selsey 9 H13
Sennen 2 J1
Sennybridge 13 D13
Settle 31 H14
Sevenoaks 10 D6
Seven Sisters 13 F12
Severn Beach 14 H4
Severn Stoke 14 B7
Sgarasta Mhor 55 H2
Sgiogarstaigh 55 A7
Shaftesbury 8 E3
Shalcombe 9 J8
Shaldon 4 F3
Shalford 9 C15
Shanklin 9 J10
Shap 31 C11
Sharnbrook 23 J8
Sharpness 14 F5
Shawbury 20 D6
Shawford 9 E9
Shebbear 3 A12
Sheerness 11 B10
Sheffield 28 F2
Shefford 16 B6
Sheigra 52 B3
Shenfield 17 F11
Shepley 27 D12
Shepshed 22 D3
Shepton Mallet 8 C1
Sherborne 5 B10
Sherborne St John 9 B11
Sherburn 33 G11
Sherburn in Elmet 28 A3
Shere 10 E1
Sherfield English 8 E7
Sherfield on Lodden 9 B11
Sheriff Hutton 33 H8
Sheringham 24 A6
Sherston 14 H7
Shiel Bridge 47 K9
Shieldaig 46 F8
Shifnal 21 F8
Shilbottle 37 C10
Shildon 32 B4
Shillingstone 8 G3
Shillington 16 B6
Shinfield 16 J2
Shipdham 24 E4
Shipley 27 B12
Shipston-on-Stour 15 C11
Shipton under Wychwood 15 E11
Shirebrook 28 H4
Shoeburyness 17 G14
Shoreham-by-Sea 10 J3
Shorwell 9 J9
Shotley Bridge 37 H10
Shotley Gate 25 M7
Shottermill 9 D13
Shottisham 25 L8
Shotts 39 D13
Shrewsbury 20 E5
Shrewton 8 C5
Shrivenham 15 H11
Siabost 55 C4
Sible Hedingham 25 M2
Sibsey 29 J12
Sidbury 4 E5
Sidford 4 E5
Sidlesham 9 H13
Sidmouth 4 E5
Silloth 35 H12
Silsden 32 K2
Silverdale 31 G10
Silverstone 16 A1
Silverton 4 C3
Simonsbath 6 H6
Singleton 9 F13
Sittingbourne 11 C10
Sixpenny Handley 8 F5
Sizewell 25 J9
Skegness 29 H14
Skellingthorpe 29 G8
Skelmersdale 26 E5
Skelmorlie 38 D6
Skelton
Cumb 31 A10
Skelton *continued*
Redcar 33 C8
Skerray 52 B8
Skinburness 35 H12
Skipness 38 E4
Skipsea 33 J13
Skipton 32 J1
Skirlaugh 29 A10
Slaidburn 31 J13
Slaithwaite 27 D11
Slaley 37 H8
Slamannan 39 C13
Sleaford 23 A9
Sledmere 33 H11
Sleights 33 D10
Sligachan 47 H4
Slough 16 H4
Smailholm 41 K9
Smarden 11 E9
Smethwick 21 H11
Smithfield 36 G3
Snainton 33 F11
Snaith 28 B5
Snape 25 K8
Sneaton 33 D10
Snettisham 24 B1
Snodland 17 J12
Soham 23 H14
Solas 54 B5
Solihull 21 H12
Solva 12 D1
Somerby 22 D6
Somercotes 28 J3
Somersham 23 H12
Somerton 7 J13
Sonning 16 H2
Sonning Common 16 H2
Sopley 8 H6
Sorbie 34 J5
Sordale 53 B13
Sorisdale 42 B4
Sorn 39 H10
Sortat 53 B14
Soulby 31 C13
Southam 22 J3
Southampton 9 F9
South Anston 28 F4
South Benfleet 17 G12
Southborough 10 E6
South Brent 3 F14
South Cave 29 A8
South Cerney 15 G9
South Elkington 29 F11
Southend 38 K1
Southend-on-Sea 17 G13
Southery 24 F1
South Harting 9 F12
South Hayling 9 H12
South Kelsey 29 E9
South Kirkby 28 C3
Southminster 17 F14
South Molton 6 J5
South Ockendon 17 G10
South Otterington 32 F5
South Petherton 5 B8
South Petherwin 3 C11
Southport 26 D4
South Shields 37 G12
South Tawton 3 B14
South Walsham 24 D8
Southwark 10 B4
South Warnborough 9 C12
Southwell 28 J5
Southwick 10 J3
Southwold 24 H10
South Woodham Ferrers 17 F13
South Wootton 24 C1
South Zeal 3 B14
Sowerby 32 F6
Sowerby Bridge 27 C11
Spalding 23 C11
Spaldwick 23 H10
Sparkford 5 A10
Spean Bridge 44 A4
Speke 26 G5
Spennymoor 32 A4
Spey Bay 50 A2
Spilsby 29 H13

Spittal . . . 12 D3
Spittal of Glenmuick . 51 J1
Spittle of Glenshee . 45 B12
Spixworth . . . 24 D7
Spofforth . . . 32 J5
Spott . . . 41 F9
Sproatley . . . 29 A10
Stadhampton . . . 16 F1
Staffin . . . 46 E4
Stafford . . . 21 D10
Staindrop . . . 32 B3
Staines-upon-
   Thames . . . 16 H5
Stainforth
   N Yorks . . . 31 H14
   S Yorks . . . 28 C5
Stainton
   Lincs . . . 29 G9
   Mbro . . . 32 C6
Staintondale . . . 33 E11
Staithes . . . 33 C9
Stalbridge . . . 5 B11
Stalham . . . 24 C8
Stallingborough . . . 29 C10
Stalybridge . . . 27 F10
Stamford . . . 23 E9
Stamford Bridge . . . 33 J9
Stamfordham . . . 37 F9
Standish . . . 26 D6
Standlake . . . 15 F12
Stanford le Hope . . . 17 G12
Stanford on Teme . . 21 K8
Stanhope . . . 37 K8
Stanley
   Durham . . . 37 H11
   Perth . . . 45 F13
Stannington . . . 37 E11
Stansted Airport . . . 17 C10
Stansted
   Mountfitchet . . . 17 C10
Stanton . . . 25 H4
Stanton Harcourt . . . 15 F13
Stanton St John . . . 15 F14
Stanway . . . 15 C9
Stanwix . . . 36 H3
Stapleford . . . 22 B3
Staplehurst . . . 11 E8
Starcross . . . 4 F3
Staunton . . . 14 D6
Staunton on Wye . . 14 B2
Staveley
   Cumb . . . 31 E10
   Derbys . . . 28 G3
Staxigoe . . . 53 C15
Staxton . . . 33 G12
Steeple Bumpstead 17 A11
Steeple Claydon . . . 16 C2
Stein . . . 46 F2
Stenhousemuir . . . 39 B13
Stenness . . . 57 E3
Stevenage . . . 16 C7
Stevenston . . . 38 F7
Stewarton . . . 39 F9
Steyning . . . 10 H2
Stibb Cross . . . 6 K3
Stichill . . . 41 K10
Stickford . . . 29 H12
Stickney . . . 29 J12
Stillington . . . 32 H7
Stilton . . . 23 G10
Stirling . . . 39 A12
Stobbs . . . 36 C4
Stobo . . . 40 K4
Stock . . . 17 F12
Stockbridge . . . 9 D8
Stockport . . . 27 F10
Stocksbridge . . . 27 F13
Stockton . . . 22 J3
Stockton-on-Tees . 32 B6
Stoer . . . 52 F2
Stoke . . . 11 B9
Stoke Albany . . . 22 G7
Stoke Ferry . . . 24 F2
Stoke Fleming . . . 4 J2
Stoke Gabriel . . . 4 H2
Stoke Mandeville . 16 E3
Stokenchurch . . . 16 F2
Stoke-on-Trent . . . 21 B9
Stoke Poges . . . 16 G4

Stoke Prior . . . 21 K10
Stokesley . . . 32 C7
Stone
   Bucks . . . 16 D2
   Glos . . . 14 G5
   Staffs . . . 21 C9
Stonehaven . . . 51 J7
Stonehouse
   Glos . . . 14 F7
   S Lanark . . . 39 F12
Stoneykirk . . . 34 H2
Stonham Aspal . . . 25 K6
Stony Stratford . . . 16 B3
Stornoway . . . 55 D6
Storrington . . . 10 H1
Stotfold . . . 16 B7
Stourbridge . . . 21 H10
Stourpaine . . . 8 G3
Stourport-on-
   Severn . . . 21 J9
Stow . . . 40 J7
Stow Bardolph . . . 24 E1
Stowmarket . . . 25 K5
Stow-on-the-Wold 15 D11
Strachan . . . 51 H5
Strachur . . . 44 J2
Stradbroke . . . 25 H7
Straiton . . . 34 C4
Stranraer . . . 34 G1
Stratford St Mary . . . 25 M5
Stratford-upon-
   Avon . . . 15 A11
Strathan . . . 52 B7
Strathaven . . . 39 F11
Strathblane . . . 39 C10
Strathdon . . . 50 F2
Strathkanaird . . . 52 H3
Strathpeffer . . . 48 C5
Strathy . . . 53 B10
Strathyre . . . 44 H7
Stratmiglo . . . 40 B5
Stratton
   Corn . . . 3 A10
   Glos . . . 15 F9
Stratton St
   Margaret . . . 15 H10
Streatley . . . 15 J14
Street . . . 7 H13
Strensall . . . 33 H8
Stretford . . . 27 F9
Stretham . . . 23 H14
Stretton
   Rutland . . . 23 D8
   Staffs . . . 21 D13
   Warr . . . 26 G7
Strichen . . . 50 B8
Stromeferry . . . 47 H8
Stromemore . . . 47 H8
Stromness . . . 56 E2
Stronachlachar . . . 44 H6
Strone . . . 38 B6
Strontian . . . 42 B10
Stroud . . . 14 F7
Struy . . . 48 D4
Stubbington . . . 9 G10
Studland . . . 8 J5
Studley . . . 21 K11
Sturminster Marshall . 8 H4
Sturminster Newton . 5 B11
Sturry . . . 11 D12
Sturton . . . 28 F7
Sudbury
   Derbys . . . 21 C12
   Suff . . . 25 L3
Sulby . . . 30 F3
Sullom . . . 57 E4
Sully . . . 7 E10
Sumburgh . . . 57 M5
Sunderland . . . 37 H13
Sunk Island . . . 29 C11
Sunninghill . . . 16 J4
Sutterton . . . 23 B11
Sutton
   Cambs . . . 23 H13
   London . . . 10 C3
Sutton Bridge . . . 23 C13
Sutton Coldfield . . . 21 G12
Sutton Courtenay . 15 G14
Sutton-in-Ashfield . 28 H3

Sutton Lane Ends . . 27 H10
Sutton-on-Sea . . . 29 F14
Sutton-on-Trent . . 28 H6
Sutton Scotney . . . 9 D9
Sutton-under-
   Whitestonecliffe . . 32 F6
Sutton Valence . . . 11 E9
Swadlincote . . . 21 E13
Swaffham . . . 24 E3
Swalcliffe . . . 15 C12
Swalecliffe . . . 11 C12
Swanage . . . 8 K5
Swanley . . . 10 C6
Swansea . . . 13 G10
Sway . . . 8 H7
Swindon . . . 15 H10
Swinefleet . . . 28 B6
Swineshead . . . 23 A11
Swinton
   Borders . . . 41 J11
   Grt Manchester . . 27 E8
   S Yorks . . . 28 E3
Symbister . . . 57 F6
Symington . . . 40 K2
Symonds Yat . . . 14 E4
Syresham . . . 16 A1
Syston . . . 22 D5

T

Tadcaster . . . 32 K6
Tadley . . . 9 A11
Tain . . . 53 K9
Talgarth . . . 13 C15
Talisker . . . 46 D9
Talley . . . 13 C10
Talsarnau . . . 18 G6
Talybont . . . 19 M6
Tal-y-llyn . . . 19 K7
Talysarn . . . 18 E4
Tamerton Foliot . . 3 F12
Tamworth . . . 21 F13
Tangmere . . . 9 G13
Tannadice . . . 51 M3
Tanworth-in-Arden 21 J12
Taobh Tuath . . . 55 J1
Tarbert . . . 38 D3
Tarbert / Aird Asaig
   Tairbeart . . . 55 G3
Tarbet
   Argyll . . . 44 J5
   Highland . . . 47 M7
Tarbolton . . . 39 H9
Tarland . . . 50 G3
Tarleton . . . 26 C5
Tarporley . . . 26 J6
Tarrant Hinton . . . 8 G4
Tarskavaig . . . 47 K5
Tarves . . . 50 D7
Tarvin . . . 26 J5
Tattenhall . . . 26 K5
Tattersett . . . 24 B3
Taunton . . . 7 J11
Tavistock . . . 3 D12
Tay Bridge . . . 40 A7
Tayinloan . . . 38 F2
Taynuilt . . . 44 F2
Tayport . . . 40 A7
Teangue . . . 47 L6
Tebay . . . 31 D12
Tedburn St Mary . . 4 D2
Teesside . . . 32 B6
Teignmouth . . . 4 F3
Telford . . . 20 F7
Temple Combe . . . 5 A11
Temple Ewell . . . 11 E13
Temple Sowerby . . 31 B12
Templeton . . . 12 E5
Tenbury Wells . . . 20 K7
Tenby . . . 12 G5
Tenterden . . . 11 F9
Terrington . . . 33 G8
Terrington St
   Clement . . . 23 C14
Tetbury . . . 14 G7
Tetney . . . 29 D12
Tetsworth . . . 16 E1
Teviothead . . . 36 C3

Tewkesbury . . . 15 C8
Teynham . . . 11 C10
Thame . . . 16 E2
Thatcham . . . 15 K14
Thaxted . . . 17 B11
Theale . . . 16 H1
The Barony . . . 56 D2
The Mumbles . . . 13 H10
Thetford . . . 24 G3
Thirsk . . . 32 F6
Thornaby on Tees . . 32 C6
Thornbury . . . 14 H5
Thorndon . . . 25 J6
Thorne . . . 28 C5
Thorney . . . 23 E11
Thornham . . . 24 A2
Thornhill
   Dumfries . . . 35 D9
   Stirling . . . 45 J8
Thornthwaite . . . 31 B8
Thornton . . . 26 A4
Thornton-le-Dale . . 33 F10
Thorpe . . . 24 E7
Thorpe-le-Soken . . 25 N6
Thorverton . . . 4 C3
Thrapston . . . 23 H8
Three Legged Cross . 8 G5
Threlkeld . . . 31 B9
Threshfield . . . 32 H1
Thrumster . . . 53 D15
Thurcroft . . . 28 F3
Thurlby . . . 23 D10
Thurlestone . . . 3 G14
Thurmaston . . . 22 E5
Thursby . . . 36 H2
Thurso . . . 53 B13
Ticehurst . . . 11 G8
Tickhill . . . 28 E4
Tideswell . . . 27 H12
Tidworth . . . 8 C7
Tighnabruaich . . . 38 C4
Tilbury . . . 17 H11
Tillicoultry . . . 40 D2
Tillingham . . . 17 E15
Tilmanstone . . . 11 E13
Timberscombe . . . 7 G8
Timsbury . . . 8 B1
Tingewick . . . 16 B1
Tingwall . . . 56 D3
Tintagel . . . 3 C8
Tintern Parva . . . 14 F4
Tipton . . . 21 G10
Tiptree . . . 25 P4
Tisbury . . . 8 E4
Titchfield . . . 9 G10
Tiverton . . . 4 B3
Toab . . . 57 L4
Toberonochy . . . 43 H9
Tobha Mor . . . 54 F4
Toddington . . . 16 C5
Todmorden . . . 27 C10
Tolastadh bho
   Thuath . . . 55 C7
Tollesbury . . . 25 Q4
Tolpuddle . . . 5 D11
Tomatin . . . 49 F9
Tomdoun . . . 48 H2
Tomintoul . . . 49 G12
Tomnavoulin . . . 49 F13
Tonbridge . . . 10 E6
Tondu . . . 13 H12
Tong . . . 21 F9
Tongue . . . 52 C7
Tonyrefail . . . 7 C9
Topcliffe . . . 32 G6
Topsham . . . 4 E3
Torbay . . . 4 H3
Torcross . . . 4 J2
Torness . . . 48 F6
Torphins . . . 50 G5
Torpoint . . . 3 F12
Torquay . . . 4 G3
Torridon . . . 46 F9
Torrible . . . 52 H7
Torthorwald . . . 35 E11
Torver . . . 31 E8
Toscaig . . . 47 H7
Totland . . . 9 J8

Totley . . . 28 F2
Totnes . . . 4 H1
Totton . . . 9 F8
Towcester . . . 16 A2
Tower Hamlets . . . 10 A4
Tow Law . . . 37 K10
Town Yetholm . . . 36 A7
Trafford Park . . . 27 F8
Tranent . . . 40 F7
Trawsfynydd . . . 18 G7
Trecastle . . . 13 D12
Tredegar . . . 13 F15
Trefeglwys . . . 19 L9
Trefnant . . . 18 C10
Trefriw . . . 18 D7
Tregaron . . . 19 Q6
Tregony . . . 2 G7
Tregynon . . . 20 G2
Treharris . . . 7 B10
Trelech . . . 12 C6
Tremadog . . . 18 G5
Trenance . . . 2 E6
Trentham . . . 21 B9
Treorchy . . . 13 G13
Tresilian . . . 2 G6
Tretower . . . 13 D15
Treuddyn . . . 26 K3
Trimdon . . . 32 A5
Trimley . . . 25 M7
Tring . . . 16 D3
Trinity . . . 5 Jersey
Troon . . . 39 G8
Troutbeck . . . 31 D10
Trowbridge . . . 8 B3
Trull . . . 7 J11
Trumpan . . . 46 E2
Trumpington . . . 23 K13
Trunch . . . 24 B7
Truro . . . 2 G6
Tuddenham . . . 25 H2
Tudweiliog . . . 18 G2
Tullynessle . . . 50 F4
Tummel Bridge . . . 45 D9
Tunstall . . . 25 K8
Turnberry . . . 34 C3
Turriff . . . 50 B6
Turvey . . . 23 K8
Tutbury . . . 21 D13
Tuxford . . . 28 G6
Twatt . . . 56 D2
Tweedmouth . . . 41 H12
Tweedshaws . . . 35 B11
Tweedsmuir . . . 35 A11
Twenty . . . 23 C10
Twyford
   Hants . . . 9 E9
   Leics . . . 22 D6
   Wokingham . . . 16 H3
Tydd St Giles . . . 23 D13
Tydd St Mary . . . 23 D13
Tylorstown . . . 7 B9
Tyndrum . . . 44 F5
Tynemouth . . . 37 G12
Ty'n-y-groes . . . 18 C7
Tywardreath . . . 3 F8
Tywyn . . . 19 K5

U

Uckfield . . . 10 G5
Uddingston . . . 39 D11
Uffculme . . . 4 B4
Uffington . . . 15 H12
Ufford . . . 25 K8
Ugborough . . . 3 F14
Uig . . . 46 E4
Ulbster . . . 53 D15
Ulceby . . . 29 C9
Ulceby Cross . . . 29 G13
Uley . . . 14 G6
Ullapool . . . 52 J3
Ulsta . . . 57 D5
Ulverston . . . 31 G8
Unapool . . . 52 E4
Upavon . . . 8 B6

Uphill . . . 7 F12
Upper Chapel . . . 13 C14
Upper Heyford . . . 15 D14
Upper Hindhope . . . 36 C6
Upper Poppleton . . . 32 J7
Upper Tean . . . 21 C11
Uppertown . . . 56 G4
Uppingham . . . 22 F7
Upton . . . 26 J5
Upton Snodsbury . . . 15 A8
Upton upon Severn . . 14 B7
Upwey . . . 5 E10
Urchfont . . . 8 B5
Urmston . . . 27 F8
Usk . . . 14 F2
Usselby . . . 29 E9
Uttoxeter . . . 21 C11
Uyeasound . . . 57 B6

V

Valley . . . 18 C2
Veness . . . 56 C5
Ventnor . . . 9 K10
Verwood . . . 8 G5
Veryan . . . 2 H7
Vickerstown . . . 30 H7
Vidlin . . . 57 F5
Virginia Water . . . 16 J5
Voe . . . 57 F5
Voy . . . 56 E2

W

Waddesdon . . . 16 D2
Waddingham . . . 29 E8
Waddington . . . 29 H8
Wadebridge . . . 2 D7
Wadhurst . . . 10 F7
Wainfleet All
Saints . . . 29 H13
Wakefield . . . 28 B2
Walberswick . . . 25 H9
Walcott . . . 29 J10
Walderslade . . . 17 J12
Waldron . . . 10 H6
Walford . . . 20 J4
Walkerburn . . . 40 K6
Walkeringham . . . 28 E6
Wallasey . . . 26 F4
Wallingford . . . 16 G1
Walls . . . 57 H3
Wallsend . . . 37 G12
Walmer . . . 11 E14
Walpole . . . 23 D13
Walsall . . . 21 G11
Walsham le Willows . 25 H4
Walsoken . . . 23 D13
Waltham . . . 29 D11
Waltham Abbey . . . 17 F8
Waltham Forest . . 17 G8
Waltham on the
Wolds . . . 22 C7
Walton . . . 36 G4
Walton-on-Thames . 10 C2
Walton-on-the-
Naze . . . 25 N7
Wanborough . . . 15 H11
Wandsworth . . . 10 B3
Wangford . . . 24 H9
Wansford . . . 23 F9
Wantage . . . 15 H13
Warboys . . . 23 G12
Wardington . . . 15 B13
Wardle . . . 26 K7
Ware . . . 17 D8
Wareham . . . 8 J4
Wargrave . . . 16 H2
Wark . . . 36 F7
Warkworth . . . 37 C11
Warley . . . 21 H11
Warminster . . . 8 C3

Warrington . . . 26 G7
Warton . . . 31 G10
Warwick . . . 22 J1
Wasbister . . . 56 C3
Washaway . . . 3 E8
Washford . . . 7 H9
Washingborough . . . 29 G9
Washington
  T&W . . . 37 H12
  W Sus. . . . 10 H2
Watchet . . . 7 G9
Watchfield . . . 15 G11
Waterbeach . . . 23 J13
Waterhead . . . 51 K3
Waterhouses . . . 21 A11
Wateringbury . . . 10 D7
Waterlooville . . . 9 G11
Watford . . . 16 F6
Wath upon Dearne . . 28 E3
Watlington
  Norf . . . 24 D1
  Oxon. . . . 16 F1
Watten . . . 53 C14
Watton . . . 24 E4
Waunfawr . . . 18 E5
Weachyburn . . . 50 B5
Wearhead . . . 36 K7
Weasenham . . . 24 C3
Weaverham . . . 26 H7
Weaverthorpe . . . 33 G11
Wedmore . . . 7 G13
Wednesbury . . . 21 G10
Wednesfield . . . 21 F10
Weedon Bec . . . 22 J5
Weeley . . . 25 N6
Welbourn . . . 29 J8
Weldon
  Northants . . . 23 G8
  Northumb . . . 37 D10
Welford
  Northants . . . 22 G5
  W Berks . . . 15 J13
Wellesbourne . . . 15 A11
Wellingborough . . 22 J7
Wellington
  Som . . . 4 B5
  Telford . . . 20 E7
Wells . . . 7 G14
Wells-next-the-Sea . 24 A4
Welney . . . 23 F14
Welshampton . . . 20 C5
Welshpool . . . 20 F3
Welton . . . 29 G9
Welwyn Garden City . 16 D7
Wem . . . 20 D6
Wembury . . . 3 G13
Wemyss Bay . . . 38 C6
Wendover . . . 16 E3
Wensley . . . 32 E3
Wenvoe . . . 7 D10
Weobley . . . 14 A3
Werrington . . . 3 C11
West Bergholt . . . 25 N4
Westbourne . . . 9 G12
West Bridgford . . . 22 B4
West Bromwich . . . 21 G11
West Burton . . . 32 F2
Westbury
  Shrops . . . 20 F4
  Wilts. . . . 8 C3
Westbury-on-
  Severn . . . 14 E6
Westbury-sub-
  Mendip. . . . 7 G14
West Calder . . . 40 G3
West Coker . . . 5 B9
Westcott . . . 10 E2
West Dean . . . 8 E7
West End . . . 9 F9
Westerham . . . 10 D5
West Felton . . . 20 D4
Westfield . . . 11 H9
West Grinstead . . . 10 G2
West Haddon . . . 22 H5
Westhill . . . 50 G7
Westhoughton . . . 26 E7
West Kilbride . . . 38 F7

West Kingsdown 10 C6
West Kirby . . . 26 G3
Westleton . . . 25 J9
West Linton . . . 40 H4
West Looe . . . 3 F10
West Lulworth . . . 8 K3
West Malling . . . 10 D7
West Meon . . . 9 E11
West Mersea . . . 25 P5
Westminster . . . 10 A4
West Moors . . . 8 G5
Weston . . . 21 D10
Weston-super-Mare. 7 E12
Westonzoyland . . . 7 H12
West Rasen . . . 29 F9
Westruther . . . 41 H9
West Thorney . . . 9 G12
Westward Ho! . . . 6 J3
West Wellow . . . 9 F8
West Woodburn . . . 36 E7
Wetheral . . . 36 H3
Wetherby . . . 32 K6
Wetwang . . . 33 J11
Weybourne . . . 24 A6
Weybridge . . . 16 J5
Weyhill . . . 9 C8
Weymouth . . . 5 F10
Whaley Bridge . . . 27 G11
Whalley . . . 27 B8
Whalton . . . 37 E10
Whatton . . . 22 B6
Whauphill . . . 34 J5
Whaw . . . 32 D1
Wheathampstead. . . 16 D6
Wheatley
  Notts . . . 28 F6
  Oxon. . . . 15 F14
Wheatley Hill . . . 37 K12
Wheaton Aston . . . 21 E9
Wheldrake . . . 33 K8
Whicham . . . 30 F7
Whickham . . . 37 G11
Whimple . . . 4 D4
Whipsnade . . . 16 D5
Whissendine . . . 22 D7
Whitburn . . . 40 G2
Whitby . . . 33 C10
Whitchurch
  Bristol . . . 14 K5
  Bucks . . . 16 D3
  Devon . . . 3 D12
  Hants . . . 9 C9
  Hereford . . . 14 E4
  Shrops . . . 20 B6
White Bridge 48 G5
Whitehall Village . . . 56 D6
Whitehaven . . . 30 C5
Whitehouse . . . 38 D3
Whitekirk . . . 41 E9
Whiteparish . . . 8 E7
Whitfield . . . 11 E14
Whithorn . . . 34 K5
Whitland . . . 12 E5
Whitley Bay . . . 37 F12
Whitonditch . . . 15 J11
Whitsome . . . 41 H11
Whitstable . . . 11 C12
Whitstone . . . 3 B10
Whittington
  Derbys . . . 28 G2
  Lancs . . . 31 G12
  Shrops . . . 20 C4
  Staffs . . . 21 F12
Whittlebury . . . 16 A1
Whittlesey . . . 23 F11
Whittlesford . . . 17 A9
Whitwell
  Derbys . . . 28 G4
  IoW . . . 9 K10
Whitwick . . . 22 D3
Whitworth . . . 27 D9
Whixley . . . 32 J6
Whome . . . 56 G3
Wick
  Hants . . . 8 F6
  Highland . . . 53 D15
  V Glam . . . 13 J13

Wicken . . . 23 H14
Wickford . . . 17 F12
Wickham . . . 9 G10
Wickham Market . . . 25 K8
Wickwar . . . 14 H6
Widdrington . . . 37 D11
Widecombe in the
  Moor. . . . 4 F1
Widemouth Bay . . . 3 A9
Wide Open . . . 37 F11
Widnes . . . 26 G6
Wigan . . . 26 E6
Wigmore
  Hereford . . . 20 K5
  Medway . . . 11 C9
Wigston . . . 22 F5
Wigton . . . 35 J13
Wigtown . . . 34 H5
Wilkhaven . . . 53 K11
Willand . . . 4 C4
Willaston . . . 26 H4
Willenhall . . . 21 F10
Willersley . . . 14 B2
Willesborough . . . 11 E11
Willingdon . . . 10 J7
Willington
  Bedford . . . 16 A6
  Durham . . . 37 K10
Williton . . . 7 H9
Willoughby . . . 29 G13
Wilmington . . . 4 D6
Wilmslow . . . 27 G9
Wilnecote . . . 21 F13
Wilton . . . 8 D6
Wimblington. . . 23 F13
Wimborne Minster . . 8 H5
Wincanton . . . 5 A11
Winchcombe . . . 15 D9
Winchelsea . . . 11 H10
Winchester . . . 9 E9
Windermere . . . 31 E10
Windsor . . . 16 H4
Windygates . . . 40 C6
Wing . . . 16 C3
Wingate . . . 37 K13
Wingham . . . 11 D13
Winkleigh. . . 3 A14
Winscombe . . . 7 F13
Winsford . . . 26 J7
Winslow . . . 16 C2
Winster . . . 27 J13
Winston . . . 32 C3
Winterborne
  Stickland . . . 8 G3
Winterbourne Abbas. 5 E10
Winterton
  N Lincs . . . 29 C8
  Norf . . . 24 C9
Wirksworth . . . 28 J1
Wisbech . . . 23 D13
Wisbech St Mary . . 23 E13
Wisborough Green . . 10 G1
Wishaw . . . 39 E13
Witchampton . . . 8 G4
Witchford. . . 23 H14
Witham . . . 17 D13
Witheridge. . . 4 B1
Withern . . . 29 F13
Withernsea . . . 29 B12
Withington. . . 15 E9
Witley . . . 9 D14
Witnesham . . . 25 K6
Witney . . . 15 E12
Wittersham . . . 11 G10
Wiveliscombe . . . 7 J9
Wivelsfield. . . 10 G4
Wivenhoe . . . 25 N5
Wix . . . 25 N6
Woburn . . . 16 B4
Woburn Sands . . . 16 B4
Woking . . . 10 C2
Wokingham . . . 16 J3
Wolf's Castle. . . 12 D3
Wollaston . . . 23 J8
Wolsingham . . . 37 K9
Wolverhampton . . . 21 G10
Wolverton . . . 16 B3

Wolviston . . . 32 B6
Wombwell . . . 28 D2
Wonersh . . . 10 E1
Wonston . . . 9 D9
Woodbridge . . . 25 L7
Woodbury . . . 4 E4
Woodchester. . . 14 F7
Woodchurch . . . 11 F10
Woodcote . . . 16 G1
Woodgreen . . . 8 F6
Woodhall Spa . . . 29 H11
Woodhouse . . . 28 F3
Woodhouse Eaves . . 22 D4
Woodley . . . 16 H2
Woodstock . . . 15 E13
Woofferton . . . 20 K6
Wookey . . . 7 G14
Wookey Hole. . . 7 G14
Wool . . . 8 J3
Woolacombe . . . 6 G3
Woolavington . . . 7 G12
Wooler . . . 37 A8
Woolwich . . . 10 B5
Woolwich Ferry . . . 10 B5
Wooperton . . . 37 A9
Woore . . . 21 B8
Wootton Bridge . . . 9 H10
Wootton Wawen. . . 21 K12
Worcester . . . 14 A7
Worfield . . . 21 G8
Workington . . . 30 B5
Worksop . . . 28 G4
Wormit . . . 40 A6
Worsbrough . . . 28 D2
Wortham . . . 24 H5
Worthing . . . 10 J2
Wotton under Edge . . 14 G6
Wragby . . . 29 G10
Wrangle . . . 29 J13
Wrea Green . . . 26 B4
Wrentham . . . 24 G9
Wretham . . . 24 G4
Wrexham . . . 20 A4
Writtle . . . 17 E11
Wroughton . . . 15 J10
Wroxham . . . 24 D7
Wroxton . . . 15 B13
Wyberton . . . 23 A11
Wye . . . 11 E11
Wylye . . . 8 D5
Wymondham
  Leics. . . . 22 D7
  Norf . . . 24 E6

Y

Yalding . . . 11 E8
Yarcombe . . . 4 C6
Yardley Hastings. . . 22 K7
Yarm . . . 32 C6
Yarmouth . . . 9 J8
Yarnton . . . 15 E13
Yarrow . . . 36 A2
Yate . . . 14 H6
Yatton . . . 7 E13
Yaxley . . . 23 F10
Yeadon . . . 27 A12
Yealmpton . . . 3 F13
Yelverton . . . 3 E13
Yeovil . . . 5 B9
Yetminster . . . 5 C9
Y Felinheli . . . 18 D5
York . . . 32 J7
Youlgreave. . . 27 J13
Yoxall . . . 21 E12
Yoxford . . . 25 J8
Ysbyty Ifan . . . 18 F8
Ysbyty Ystwyth . . . 19 N7
Ystalyfera . . . 13 F11
Ystradgynlais . . . 13 E11

Z

Zennor . . . 2 H2